T0029073

REDISCOVER YOUR
WISDOM

Drawing on Answers from Your Past to Achieve Self-improvement, Growth, and Success

RABBI JOEL STEIN

To request permissions, contact the author at rabbistein@rediscoveryourwisdom.com

This is a work of creative nonfiction. The events are portrayed to the best of the author's memory. Some names, identifying characteristics, and details in some anecdotes and stories have been changed to protect the identities of the persons involved.

First published in 2023 by NewType Publishing

NewType Publishing
1805 Hilltop Dr Ste 211
Redding, California, 96002

Paperback ISBN: 979-8-9898664-0-3
eBook ISBN: 979-8-9898664-1-0
Library of Congress Control Number: 2024900987

Cover and book design by Allan Nygren

Printed in the United States of America

CONTENTS

INTRODUCTION
THE FAMILIAR
AND THE
FORGOTTEN

Life is a journey, filled with peaks and valleys that test our resilience, often flooding our minds with negative thoughts. But here's an incredible truth that often goes unnoticed: many of the challenges we're grappling with today are ones we've already overcome before. Think about it: how often have you found yourself trapped in doubts and fears, convinced they're insurmountable? Surprisingly, you've encountered these very struggles in the past, even if the memories have faded. The key lies in our innate ability to unravel the threads of negativity.

This realization dawned on me while assisting people in navigating their own dilemmas. As a rabbi within the Orthodox Jewish community, I've had the opportunity to meet with people in distressing situations and help them traverse through the darkness and into the light of clarity. Through mediating hundreds of disputes and inspiring hope in many a weary soul, I've come to discover common threads within the problems people face in their daily lives. I started asking, "Have you faced these thoughts before?" Frequently, the response was a puzzled look, signaling the haze of forgetfulness. Yet, as we continued our conversation, a pattern emerged: these troubling thoughts that held them captive today had visited them earlier, and incredibly, they'd managed to move past them.

A defining moment occurred when I probed, "What helped these thoughts fade away previously?" Though the specifics often slipped their minds, a common thread wove through their stories. Each person could recollect a thought or insight that had dispelled the negativity. It was as though, without realizing, they had become their own guides, equipped with the wisdom to find their way to brighter horizons.

This revelation led me to a deep understanding: the path to enduring serenity doesn't solely rely on external advice. Instead, it's deeply intertwined with our reservoir of personal experiences. So, our journey underwent a transformation—from seeking solutions outwardly to reconnecting with the thoughts that once steered us toward resolutions from within. This bond gains even greater strength when we not only revisit those thoughts but also preserve them in writing. These insights then become tools, ready to combat the recurrence of negativity.

And thus, my mission began—to capture this phenomenon, weaving together insights from a spectrum of human stories. Each chapter of this book unravels a glimpse into challenges that mirror our everyday lives. Through these narratives, you'll witness individuals dismantling their own negativity, only to see those victories fade into the backdrop of memory.

What's intriguing is that our collective journey will unveil a common pattern: your past self holds the key to your present challenges. Our exploration isn't about mere introspection—it's a voyage into your own history, to extract pearls of wisdom that can illuminate your way forward.

As we embark on this odyssey, you'll discover an array of insights that can spark your efforts to reclaim forgotten strategies, build resilience, and sow seeds of hope within the fertile soil of memory. We'll traverse a landscape where each story transforms into a guiding light, leading you toward your own moments of triumph.

Moreover, the stories that unfold aren't just stories; they're riveting and dramatic accounts of the human experience. They paint a portrait of struggle and victory that transcends boundaries of time and culture. Each story serves as a brushstroke on the canvas of life, creating a masterpiece that resonates with the core of human strength.

Throughout this voyage, you'll walk alongside individuals who, like you, have faced inner battles. You'll witness how they grappled with negativity, stumbled, and ultimately conquered. But here's where the twist emerges—a twist you've likely encountered in your own life. The twist is simple: you've walked this path before, even if the memory has faded. You've wrestled with these challenges and emerged victorious, yet the recollection of your triumphs might have dimmed over time. However, within these pages, the stories of shared success will echo with your personal victories, motivating you to rekindle those dormant strategies.

As we journey through these stories, we'll unveil rich insights. By the time we reach our destination, you'll stand armed with the knowledge that your personal history houses a treasury of strategies to conquer adversity.

In closing, I want to emphasize that this book is not just about harnessing your own past solutions; you'll also discover new strategies and techniques to solve everyday problems. These insights are drawn from my vast experience working with people who struggled with life's problems, including cases that even experts gave up on. Despite the odds, my approach consistently defied expectations and achieved success.

Join me on this expedition into the familiar and the forgotten. Together, we'll dive deep into the sea of your experiences, emerging with pearls of wisdom that will guide you through life's challenges. By learning from our past selves, we can illuminate the path ahead and forge a brighter, more resilient future.

PART 1

FORTIFY
YOUR
IDENTITY

CHAPTER 1
ELEVATE YOUR SELF-ESTEEM

Overcome Self-Doubt through Radical Self-Acceptance

How we perceive ourselves and our identities is shaped by our level of self-esteem. Self-esteem isn't about mere self-confidence or ego. It's a deep understanding of one's intrinsic value and potential. It's the belief that despite challenges, setbacks, or negative influences, you possess the capability to rise above and achieve your aspirations. Just as oxygen fuels our physical existence, self-esteem fuels our mental and emotional well-being.

In essence, self-esteem is the driving force behind not only personal accomplishments but also the resilience required to overcome obstacles. It's the bedrock upon which self-improvement, growth, and success are built. So, when considering the importance of self-esteem, it's crucial to remember that fostering a positive self-image isn't just beneficial—it's vital for unlocking the doors to a fulfilling life.

By pursuing personal acceptance, we engage in an exploration of our intrinsic worth, challenging the limiting beliefs that impede our growth. Through the lens of radical self-acceptance, we'll explore the

transformative potential embedded in the deliberate choice to cultivate self-love and self-honor, illuminating a path toward heightened
self-esteem and a more fulfilling existence.

Reshape Your Narrative

A person came to me carrying the heavy burden of low self-esteem, a
weight that had tethered him for years. Within his story lay a pivotal
chapter etched with the memory of a teacher who had relentlessly
chipped away at his self-worth. The teacher's words, like daggers, had
consistently struck, leaving behind wounds that time had struggled
to heal. This story was an anchor to his self-doubt, an anchor he was
eager to release.

As he recounted his experiences, the power of that teacher's verbal
abuse became evident. But hidden within his retelling were moments
of quiet resistance. These were the instances when he had defied the
teacher's negative narrative, when he had consciously countered the
toxicity with a precise thought: "My teacher is a bumbling fool."

These moments were, however, fleeting. Overwhelmed by the
weight of negativity, he had forgotten this powerful tool he had crafted
for himself. It was a forgotten treasure, a gem buried beneath layers
of doubt and pain.

With a guiding hand, I urged him to recall these moments, these
instances when he had held his own against the storm of criticism.
And so, we embarked on a journey of introspection, exploring those
forgotten pockets of resilience. Amid the shadows, he began to recognize the light that his own thought had provided. It was a realization
that carried with it a spark of hope.

I presented a question that invited reflection: if he were to face a professional challenge, like negotiating a raise with his boss, would he seek advice from this very teacher, the one he had labeled a "bumbling fool"? Laughter bubbled forth as he contemplated the absurdity of relying on someone he considered intellectually deficient. In a candid moment, he shared his lack of respect for the teacher's judgment, cementing the incongruity of letting such an individual dictate his self-worth. The realization dawned that he had entrusted his self-esteem to someone he dismissed as lacking competence. The paradox was stark, and in its starkness lay the key to his liberation.

With this insight, I encouraged him to reconnect with his forgotten tool, the affirmation that had shielded him from the teacher's negative influence. "My teacher's opinions hold no weight; he lacks competence. I wouldn't even consider seeking advice from him about minor matters." This affirmation crystallized his resistance, a counterweight to the teacher's destructive words.

The journey that followed was one of diligence and self-discovery. He adopted the affirmation into his daily routine, a conscious reminder of his own resilience. The fog of self-doubt began to lift. Slowly but surely, he learned to embrace this weapon he had crafted himself. The affirmation became a guiding star, steering him away from the pitfalls of doubt and despair. With each passing day, he found himself shedding the weight of the teacher's negative influence, stepping into a new narrative of self-belief.

Empowered by the rediscovery of his own strength, he ventured into new territory. He pursued opportunities that once seemed out of reach, defying the limitations imposed by his past. The story that had once anchored him now propelled him forward. And so, with his self-worth reclaimed, he embarked on a journey of self-discovery, armed with the knowledge that within himself lay the strength to silence even the loudest echoes of negativity.

We all have the ability to shape our own narrative; we can either use the hurtful words others have spoken to us or we can access the self-belief within us to filter everything through. When hurtful words from others make you doubt yourself, think back to times when those words didn't bother you as much. You can rediscover the comforting thoughts that helped calm your feelings. Writing them down and keeping them in mind will help you reinforce your memory and feel more empowered.

Imagine self-esteem as the foundation upon which success is built. Just as a building's stability relies on a solid foundation, an individual's achievements rest upon a strong sense of self-worth. When self-esteem is lacking, the desire to pursue success withers away. Why would someone invest time and effort in their goals if they genuinely believe that failure is their destiny?

Consider a talented artist who creates stunning masterpieces. Their talents alone aren't enough; they must recognize and acknowledge their artistic abilities to channel them effectively. Similarly, recognizing our own capabilities empowers us to leverage our skills and seize opportunities even in the face of criticism and negativity.

Reflect on the narrative you tell yourself. Is it marked by the criticisms of others? Or is it built through your strong self-belief and acknowledgment of your talents? No matter where you are or what's been said about you, you have the power within yourself to change the narrative and rewrite your story as one of triumph and to prove the critics wrong.

Here are some questions to help you get started on rewriting your narrative:

1. What is a criticism that limits your belief in yourself?
2. Who said it and what is their relation to you?
3. How long ago did this happen? How have you changed since then?
4. How well did this person know you? What are their credentials to make them a trustworthy judge?
5. Is it possible that, in being yourself, you triggered an insecurity that they then took out on you?
6. What is the other side of their criticism? If you were to defend yourself now, how might you counter their remark?

Through literally rewriting this story out, you will have solid evidence to come back to and remind yourself of whenever this criticism comes back to haunt you. The faster you can overcome the negative beliefs that stem from this experience, the more opportunities you'll be able to take advantage of and the more you'll be able to accomplish.

Build a Foundation of Support

Childhood scars have a lasting impact that can be difficult to overcome. The foundation of these scars often begins during our formative years, when children absorb information like sponges. Children lack the cognitive filters that adults possess, making them susceptible to accepting everything they hear, whether it's positive or negative.

Encouraging words and positive affirmations are like seeds planted in fertile soil, blossoming into self-confidence and a healthy self-image. Conversely, the weight of negativity, harsh criticism, or hurtful words can dig deep roots, leaving emotional scars that persist into adulthood.

In essence, the echoes of childhood experiences reverberate throughout our lives. Recognizing the power of words and actions on young minds is a fundamental step toward nurturing well-rounded individuals. Parents hold the power to mold self-esteem and resilience through the delicate balance of affirmation and advice. This orchestrated interplay results in confident individuals who approach life with a strong sense of self and a readiness to overcome obstacles.

A harmonious blend of support and guidance is essential in creating an environment where children thrive. It's crucial for children to feel cherished and appreciated for their accomplishments, regardless of the size of those accomplishments. This equilibrium nurtures a sense of security and empowerment that serves as a resilient foundation for navigating life's challenges.

Once, a highly accomplished lawyer embarked on an unexpected journey—one that led him to the confines of a prison, where inmates were serving sentences for grave offenses. Amidst the somber surroundings, a curious prisoner mustered the courage to ask the lawyer the secret behind his remarkable success. The lawyer's response held a key to understanding the trajectory of human achievement: "My father always saw untapped potential within me, frequently expressing his belief that I would emerge as a prominent lawyer. His unwavering faith in my capabilities ignited a fire within me, propelling me to fulfill that vision."

The prisoner, intrigued by this revelation, couldn't help but contrast his own upbringing. With a hint of irony, he shared his personal experience: "My father's words took a markedly different path. He consistently predicted that I would find myself within the walls of a prison one day."

There is power vested in parental beliefs, and they wield marked influence over our destinies. Parental encouragement, or lack thereof, can mold our aspirations, expectations, and trajectories. The lawyer's journey from potential to fruition underscores the lasting influence of nurturing positive beliefs and aspirations in our children. In a world where individuals forge their paths amidst the echoes of both encouragement and skepticism, this narrative underscores the pivotal role parents play in shaping the lives of their children. It encourages parents to be mindful of the words they choose to sow in the fertile soil of their child's mind. By instilling faith, optimism, and support, they can be the architects of dreams fulfilled and lives transformed.

In my journey, I was fortunate to have a father who consistently championed my potential. A revered presence in the Jewish Orthodox community, with tens of thousands of people tuning into his weekly lectures to gain some inspiration and advice, my dad has always been an inspiration to me. As a life coach, business coach, and couples counselor, he has spent over three decades advising thousands of individuals with mental problems, helping numerous entrepreneurs pioneer multi-million-dollar businesses, and assisting people in finding effective ways to communicate in their relationships. His unwavering words of affirmation still echo in my ears: "Joel, your brilliance holds the promise of enriching society through your extraordinary gifts." These uplifting words of encouragement have proven to be a compass guiding me through life's adventures.

As I stand at the age of thirty-seven years old, I reflect on the remarkable trajectory of my life. By the time I reached twenty-two, I had delivered impactful lectures on halachic rulings that resonated with thousands. Additionally, I authored bestselling books that comprehensively explored the wisdom of the entire Talmud. These achievements stand as a testament to the power of early encouragement.

The story that unfolds within these pages further attests to the incredible outcomes born from establishing self-belief. As you read this book, ponder its message, and find your life reshaped, I may find no greater achievement than touching your journey through these words. If this book has the power to alter the course of your life, it could very well be my most significant accomplishment yet.

There is immeasurable value in nurturing young minds with positivity and faith. It exemplifies how a foundation of support can propel individuals to explore their potential and accomplish feats that ripple across various domains. By celebrating the potential within every young person, we contribute to a brighter future—one defined by growth, fulfillment, and purpose.

One of the most powerful tools I provide parents to nurture their children's self-esteem, especially among the younger kids, is the art of indirect praise. This method involves engaging in a telephone conversation with someone else and deliberately incorporating positive comments about your child, all while creating the illusion that they're not within earshot. This subtle yet effective approach can significantly boost the child's self-image. Moreover, openly voicing genuine compliments in the presence of others can substantially enhance their self-confidence and self-worth. By adopting these strategies, parents can actively nurture a strong foundation of self-esteem, empowering their children with the emotional resilience and self-assuredness needed to navigate life's various challenges with confidence.

Elevating your self-esteem requires a foundation of support; some people grow up with their parents being this foundation of support for them, while other people did not get that support from their parents, so they must build it now in adulthood with the help of trusted friends and advisers. This requires introspection to unearth the damage done to your self-esteem during your formative years and realize your power in believing in yourself more than anyone believed in you. It also requires surrounding yourself with positive influences who are able to uplift and encourage you in your endeavors.

I've found what helps the most is writing out any negative criticism that comes up during your introspection. Then in a list next to those criticisms, write down specific accomplishments or abilities that counteract and contradict that negative comment. Providing yourself with evidence of your own abilities and beliefs can help reverse the damage done by not having a foundation of support when you were younger. Build a case for your self-belief and be the support for yourself that you needed when you were younger.

Unlock Your Potential

In the realm of human potential, there exist untapped capabilities waiting to be awakened. Such was the case when I encountered an individual whose remarkable memory lay hidden beneath layers of self-doubt. This encounter not only shed light on the intricate relationship between belief and ability but also underscored the transformative power of a change in perspective.

This story unfolds with a man who possessed an extraordinary capacity for memory, a gift he remained completely oblivious to. Amid his pursuit of Talmudic studies, he consistently downplayed his achievements, asserting that his memory was akin to a sieve, retaining nothing of significance. The dichotomy between his latent potential and his perception of it was puzzling, and I felt compelled to explore this phenomenon further.

During one of our conversations, which revolved around the topic of memory and its role in personal growth, I probed into his conviction about his own memory capacity. I inquired if he could recollect any instances when he did remember something, even if those instances were sparse. To my surprise, he reiterated his inability to remember any substantial information from his studies.

This admission piqued my interest, leading me to dig deeper into the root cause of this cognitive dissonance. Our exploration ventured into his past, unearthing significant experiences that left a lasting imprint on his self-perception. A poignant narrative emerged, revealing that during his formative years, a figure he revered deeply subjected him to relentless criticism. The impact of these negative remarks was intense, chipping away at his self-esteem and implanting the belief that he was inherently forgetful.

Armed with this newfound understanding, I invited him to question the validity of his self-imposed limitations. I encouraged him to consider that perhaps his memory had been functioning all along, concealed by a cloud of disbelief. Our conversation took an intriguing turn as we discussed the potential influence of his beliefs on his memory retention. The intersection between psychology and memory intrigued me—how thoughts and emotions can mold memory and vice versa.

Intrigued by this insight, we decided to put his memory to the test. I posed a question from the Talmud and discreetly activated a timer. As he contemplated the answer, he was oblivious to the ticking seconds. Ten seconds elapsed, and he conceded defeat. Little did he know that his initial resignation had taken hold within a mere ten seconds. I unveiled the timing experiment, revealing that his lack of faith in his memory had sabotaged his efforts almost instantly.

With this revelation, a spark of curiosity ignited within him. I proposed a fresh approach: What if he suspended his preconceived notions about his memory? What if he momentarily set aside the notion that he was forgetful and allowed himself to engage in the challenge with an open mind? Skepticism mingled with hope in his eyes as he agreed to this experiment.

As he closed his eyes and inhaled a deep breath, a sense of determination radiated from him. I presented the same question from the Talmud, and time seemed to stretch as he grappled with the challenge. Minutes passed, and he remained immersed in thought. Just shy of the two-minute mark, he emerged from his contemplation with a smile and confidently rattled off the answer. The transformation was palpable—he had dismantled his self-imposed barriers and uncovered his latent memory capabilities.

Our exploration didn't end there; in fact, it marked a new beginning. Throughout the night, we engaged in a stimulating discourse as I fired one Talmudic question after another. His responses were astoundingly accurate and insightful. The discrepancy between his perceived forgetfulness and his demonstrated memory prowess was staggering, highlighting the deep influence of belief on human potential.

There is a strong connection between psychological disposition and capability. What we believe about ourselves either unlocks our potential or limits it. This story mirrored the broader human experience, wherein self-doubt can eclipse dormant talents waiting to be harnessed. Self-belief shapes our personal capabilities, and self-perception plays a crucial role in realizing potential. Moreover, this story serves as a testament to the malleability of human cognition, illustrating the transformative effect of an altered mindset.

As I reflect on this story, I am reminded of the human capacity for growth, and the remarkable potential that resides within each of us. It is a reminder that our beliefs, however deeply ingrained, can be challenged and recalibrated to unlock hidden reservoirs of talent. The story of unearthing an undiscovered memory highlights the winding journey of self-discovery, one that empowers us to transcend perceived limitations and reach new heights of achievement. It invites us to question the narratives we hold about ourselves and to consider how our beliefs shape our lives and stories. With a shift in perspective, dormant talents can emerge from the shadows, paving the way for extraordinary accomplishments that were once deemed impossible.

Through a combination of thoughtful dialogue and the willingness to confront misconceptions, this individual embarked on a journey of reclaiming his self-perceived lack of clarity and embracing the depth of his intellectual abilities. A revelation dawned upon me: individuals with low self-esteem often possess a remarkable abundance of talent. It's important to emphasize that not every talented individual has low self-esteem, but a noteworthy observation is that a substantial number of those grappling with self-esteem issues also harbor noteworthy talents. This observation has proven to be particularly insightful in my interactions with individuals struggling with low self-esteem. When I presented this realization to them and they began to acknowledge its validity, a palpable shift occurred in their self-perception, boosting their self-esteem.

This discovery highlights the intricate interplay between self-perception and innate abilities. It's a reminder that beneath the surface of self-doubt often lies an array of untapped talents waiting to be recognized. By recognizing this connection, we empower individuals to embrace their inherent capabilities and work toward cultivating a healthier self-esteem that is grounded in their talents and potential.

Embrace Yourself Fully

In my circle of friends, there exists a remarkable individual whose demeanor serves as a striking illustration of the impact that a robust self-esteem can have. Despite grappling with the challenge of excess weight, his self-assuredness acts as a shield against societal pressures and personal insecurities, allowing him to disarm even the most sensitive topics with his wit and confidence.

This unique trait was on full display during a memorable gathering we attended together. Amid the spirited conversations and laughter, his phone rang, his wife's voice echoing through the device. Curious about his experience, she inquired about the gathering. In a moment that drew the attention of those around us, he responded with a joviality that filled the room, "You won't believe it, dear! We're having a fantastic time, and guess what? We've got a one-man band here!" As the crowd leaned in, his wife probed for more information about the musical entertainer. With a twinkle in his eye and a grin that revealed his readiness to share a delightful secret, he replied, "Well, I happen to be the one-man band. Can you imagine? I've orchestrated my very own 'stomach band' performance!" The room erupted in hearty laughter, a collective release of joy spurred by his audacious humor.

What distinguishes him is not just his ability to see himself through a lens of self-acceptance but his capacity to invite others into that positive perspective. He embodies the concept that self-esteem isn't merely an internal experience; it's a force that shapes how we interact with the world around us. In a culture that often places an excessive emphasis on physical appearance, his demeanor acts as a beacon of authenticity and empowerment. By embracing his own physicality and skillfully weaving humor into the narrative, he highlights the sway that self-assurance and a positive self-image can have on one's outlook.

The journey toward self-esteem isn't about striving for perfection but learning to embrace our uniqueness, even if it challenges societal norms. His ability to laugh at himself resonates far beyond that one moment—it serves as a timeless reminder that self-esteem enables us to transcend societal expectations, find joy in our true selves, and positively affect those around us.

Embracing ourselves fully, despite deviations from societal norms, is a powerful act of self-affirmation that not only strengthens our self-esteem but also serves as an empowering example for others navigating similar paths. When we wholeheartedly accept our unique qualities, quirks, and differences, we send a message that authenticity is not only permissible but encouraged. In demonstrating the beauty of embracing our individuality, we contribute to creating a more inclusive and accepting environment where everyone feels empowered to be their true selves without fear of judgment or conformity to external expectations.

Become Rubber, Not Glue

Low self-esteem can significantly affect how you react to criticism. When faced with criticism, individuals with low self-esteem often respond with heightened emotional reactions. They might explode in anger at the person providing the critique, regardless of the validity of the criticism. Alternatively, they might spiral into a state of depression, leading to self-directed negativity and emotional turmoil.

Two colleagues were employed at the same company and shared a unique encounter. One particular day, the boss stormed into the office wearing a visible cloud of frustration. He wasted no time in venting his dissatisfaction, delivering a barrage of harsh comments that left his employees reeling. He disparaged their contributions, labeling them as worthless and attributing the downfall of his business to their incompetence. Surprisingly, the two employees displayed remarkably distinct reactions to the boss's tirade.

One of the workers absorbed the boss's cutting remarks like a sponge, internalizing the harsh critique and feeling deeply wounded. His self-esteem plummeted as he grappled with the perception of his own inadequacy. In stark contrast, the other employee appeared unfazed by the boss's verbal onslaught, responding with a nonchalant laugh as if the comments held no weight.

Baffled by their differing responses, the employee who had been hurt approached his coworker who seemed untroubled. With genuine curiosity, he inquired, "I'm struggling to understand how you could brush off the boss's words so easily, while I felt as though he had struck me to the core."

The coworker replied with a thoughtful smile: "It's really quite straightforward. I'm acutely aware of my own worth and capabilities, and I recognize that the boss's comments are far from accurate. On the other hand, it seems that you've internalized the belief that you're somehow lacking in value. When the boss called you worthless, it essentially echoed the doubts you already had about yourself. It's almost as if you were secretly hoping he wouldn't uncover your perceived 'worthlessness' quite so soon."

The conversation provided insight into the power of self-perception and its influence on one's emotional response to criticism. It served as a reminder that our own beliefs about ourselves can significantly color the way we perceive external feedback, and it highlighted the importance of cultivating healthy self-esteem to counter such effects.

When someone unfairly criticizes you and you know that you are not at fault, it's crucial not to take it to heart. Let me share another story to illustrate this concept. There was a professor—let's name him Peter Jones—who was an expert in human behavior. One day, during his lecture, a disturbed individual bursts into the classroom, demanding to know if he's Professor Jones. Upon confirming the professor's identity, the person unexpectedly slaps him across the face. The entire class is shocked and curious about how Professor Jones will react. To everyone's surprise, he responds with a smile and calmly says, "That's your problem."

This story teaches us a valuable lesson. Just like Professor Jones, when you encounter unjust criticism from your partner or anyone else, it's important not to internalize it. Instead of letting it affect your self-esteem, remember that the criticism may be coming from their own issues or insecurities. By adopting the mindset of "That's your problem," you can prevent unnecessary emotional turmoil and maintain your own emotional well-being.

The key takeaway here is to detach yourself from baseless criticism and remain confident in your own understanding of the situation. This not only safeguards your mental and emotional health but also contributes to a healthier and more harmonious relationship. When you become rubber instead of glue, whatever baseless criticism comes your way merely bounces off of you, ensuring the unfounded criticism doesn't stick to you and become part of your identity.

Self-Esteem Affects Your View of Others

Someone came to me describing their father's tendency to become agitated and to perceive everyone as foolish and unintelligent. If family members didn't complete tasks as he saw fit, he labeled them as lacking common sense. This created turmoil within the family. After meeting the father, I explained to him that his perception of others as foolish stemmed from not recognizing his own brilliance. By seeing himself as average, anyone who struggled to understand something he could easily understand seemed below average to him.

I suggested to the father that acknowledging his intellect and comprehension skills as above-average would prevent him from deeming those around him as unintelligent. Rather than being unable to grasp simple concepts, they merely struggled with more intricate ones, unlike him. The concepts only appear to be simple to him because of his above-average intelligence. By elevating his self-perception from average to above-average, he could help elevate those around him from below average to just average. His life and the life of his family improved as a result.

Recently, one of my well-known friends contacted me to ask for a good quote related to low self-esteem. He needed it for a significant speech he was preparing on the subject. At first, despite having crafted numerous quotes over the years, I couldn't recall any suitable ones. However, after a moment, I suddenly remembered a recent conversation with an individual who struggled with low self-esteem. During that conversation, I had spontaneously formulated a quote that I thought might be relevant. The quote went something like the following: "Why do you doubt everything in life but you are certain that you are worthless?" I shared this quote with my friend, and he expressed his satisfaction with it.

A person with a healthy self-esteem tends to exhibit a more positive outlook on life, driven by two key factors. Firstly, they possess a positive mindset that stems from viewing themselves in a favorable light, acknowledging their inherent talents and strengths. This positive self-perception acts as a foundation for their overall optimism as they recognize the value they bring to various aspects of their life. By acknowledging their abilities, they cultivate a sense of self-worthiness that permeates their interactions and experiences.

Secondly, their belief in their own abilities instills a can-do attitude, enabling them to wholeheartedly embrace various endeavors. Even if initial attempts fall short, their self-assuredness propels them to tackle challenges head-on, confident in their capability to overcome obstacles and achieve their objectives. This mindset encourages a proactive approach to life, where they willingly take on new challenges and explore uncharted territories. This attitude often leads to the accumulation of positive experiences, as they make their way through difficulties with determination.

Furthermore, the inherent belief in their capacity to handle setbacks helps them maintain resilience in the face of adversity. When confronted with obstacles, they don't succumb to defeat; instead, they brainstorm innovative solutions and adapt their strategies. This commitment to problem-solving further enriches their positive experiences, as they overcome hurdles and emerge stronger.

In contrast, individuals burdened by low self-esteem are more inclined to harbor pessimism. Their self-perception is tainted by a sense of inadequacy, causing them to believe they lack the necessary skills and talents. Consequently, they may shy away from taking on new challenges, convinced that their efforts will be futile. Even if they do venture into unfamiliar territory, their lack of self-confidence may lead them to surrender at the first sign of difficulty, convinced that their failure is inevitable. This self-defeating attitude robs them of the chance to amass positive experiences, as they're less likely to persevere through setbacks or seek out alternative solutions.

A healthy self-esteem fuels a positive mindset and a belief in one's abilities, contributing to a life rich in positive experiences. Conversely, low self-esteem often results in a negative outlook and a tendency to avoid challenges, limiting the potential for positive encounters. By recognizing the power of self-esteem on one's outlook, individuals can work toward nurturing a healthy sense of self-worth and creating a more positive, fulfilling life.

CHAPTER 2
RECOGNIZE THE POWER OF POSITIVITY

*Displace Negativity by Reminding
Yourself of All That's Good*

Cultivating a positive mindset in the face of life's challenges and uncertainties holds significance in establishing mental and emotional well-being. Regularly acknowledging and appreciating the positive aspects of one's life not only provides a counterbalance to negative thoughts but also nurtures a sense of gratitude and contentment. This intentional shift in focus empowers individuals to navigate difficulties with a more optimistic perspective, enhancing their ability to cope with adversity and maintain emotional equilibrium. Moreover, the ripple effect of a positive mindset extends to interpersonal relationships, as individuals radiate positivity and contribute to creating a more uplifting and supportive community. But it starts with a positive self-image and extends outward.

In the previous chapter, we delved into the significance of cultivating a healthy self-esteem. This trait not only shapes one's positive outlook but also paves the way for a life rich with positive experiences. A robust self-esteem serves as a catalyst, propelling individuals to take on new challenges and embrace opportunities with the unwavering belief in their capabilities. Such confidence fuels their determination to succeed, even in the face of obstacles, as they are armed with the conviction that they possess the skills to surmount any hurdle.

Undoubtedly, a healthy self-esteem generates a ripple effect that reverberates across various facets of life. When an individual becomes accustomed to adopting a positive outlook in one arena, it tends to permeate into other aspects of their life. This psychological phenomenon stems from the mind's propensity to become conditioned toward positivity. The act of consistently looking on the bright side, even within a confined context, triggers a transformative process that spills over into an overall positive mindset.

Look at the Bigger Picture

On the subject of adopting a positive perspective, a notable encounter comes to mind—one with a highly accomplished accountant. He candidly shared with me a particularly distressing day he had experienced. The narrative revolved around an individual who treated him with utter disdain, subjecting him to a verbal tirade that left him feeling belittled and disheartened. I probed further, inquiring about the duration of this disheartening episode. His response was succinct: it had spanned roughly fifteen minutes.

Drawing parallels and highlighting the stark contrast, I posed another query: how did the remainder of his day unfold? With a touch of amusement, he admitted that, on the whole, his day had been rather positive. Seizing this revelation, I playfully remarked that, given his assessment of having endured a miserable day, I might think twice about entrusting him with my accounting matters. After all, each day is comprised of twenty-four hours, not a mere fifteen minutes. It became apparent that his ability to gauge his day's overall quality was somewhat disproportionate, given the brevity of the negative encounter.

In this anecdote lies a nugget of wisdom—a reminder that our perception of our day is profoundly influenced by how we allow fleeting instances to color our overall outlook. The art of cultivating positivity involves recognizing the power of perspective. Just as a prism refracts light into a spectrum of colors, we possess the ability to infuse our daily experiences with a spectrum of positivity. Choosing to focus on the uplifting aspects and reframing the less favorable ones can transform the way we experience life's challenges.

In essence, the lesson from this episode underscores the significance of resilience in the face of adversity. It serves as a testament to our capability to insulate ourselves from momentary setbacks, allowing them to occupy the mere fringes of our perception rather than overshadowing our entire day. This approach bolsters our mental fortitude and strengthens our resilience against negativity, enabling us to greet each day with renewed optimism.

By anchoring ourselves in this perspective, we not only enhance our individual well-being but also foster a positive atmosphere that reverberates within our spheres of influence. Our disposition becomes a light illuminating the path toward embracing life's challenges with a spirit of unwavering positivity. In doing so, we transform ourselves into purveyors of optimism, cultivating an environment where even the most fleeting setbacks can't overshadow the brilliance of our positive outlook.

I once encountered an individual who was overwhelmed by the myriad challenges that seemed to be cascading into his life. It appeared that everything was going awry, and he found himself sinking into a sea of negativity. In an attempt to provide him with a fresh perspective, I suggested a simple yet transformative exercise.

I encouraged him to grab a pen and paper and create two distinct columns. In the first column, I instructed him to meticulously jot down every single thing that was currently going wrong in his life. The second column, on the other hand, was to be reserved for enumerating all the positive aspects and blessings that he had, no matter how big or small.

Upon completing this exercise, something remarkable transpired. As he reviewed the two columns side by side, he was taken aback by the disparity between them. What initially felt like a barrage of problems had now been juxtaposed with a plethora of good things, each representing a ray of light amid the shadows. It was an epiphany that his perspective had been skewed by his focus on the challenges, obscuring the goodness that was also present.

This exercise serves as a reminder of the power of perspective. Often, in the throes of life's troubles, we become ensnared in a tunnel vision that magnifies our problems while diminishing our blessings. This skewed outlook can leave us feeling overwhelmed, as if the challenges are all-consuming. However, by consciously redirecting our focus and acknowledging the positive elements, we can recalibrate our perspective.

In a way, this exercise is akin to adjusting the lens through which we view our lives. Just as a camera lens can either zoom in to capture minute details or zoom out to encompass the entire scene, we too have the ability to zoom out from our challenges and take in the broader panorama of our lives. Doing so allows us to recognize that while setbacks may exist, they are just a part of the grand tapestry that also includes moments of joy, achievements, relationships, and a myriad of blessings.

This exercise need not be a one-time occurrence. It can become a dynamic tool that we turn to whenever life's storms cloud our vision. By revisiting our list of positive experiences, we can rekindle the sense of balance and equilibrium that often eludes us during challenging times. This isn't about denying or dismissing our difficulties; it's about contextualizing them within the larger framework of our lives.

In essence, the act of listing both the challenges and the blessings serves as an embodiment of the age-old adage, "Count your blessings." It's a practice that encourages us to acknowledge the silver linings, however faint they may seem at times. Through this exercise, we realize that despite life's inevitable hurdles, we possess a capacity of goodness that is often overshadowed by the transient clouds of adversity.

So, the next time life's challenges threaten to consume your thoughts, consider taking a moment to create those two columns. As you document the good and the not-so-good, you may find yourself, like my acquaintance, pleasantly surprised by the abundant goodness that resides in the shadows of life's challenges.

Practice Gratitude

In a touching encounter, I had the privilege of observing a person who had stared into the abyss of death, only to emerge from it with a deep sense of joy and appreciation for life. This experience left me contemplating the intricate dance between gratitude and complacency that characterizes the human spirit.

In this powerful moment, I was introduced to two individuals—one who had battled against the clutches of mortality and emerged victorious and another who enjoyed the gift of a healthy heart without facing such a harrowing ordeal. What struck me most was the stark contrast in their levels of happiness and gratitude.

The survivor of the cardiac arrest exuded an undeniable aura of happiness, a palpable energy that radiated from within. His smile was infectious, a testament to his newfound zest for life. It puzzled me initially: why was someone who had faced the fragility of life more content than the person who enjoyed the steady rhythm of a healthy heart?

Upon deeper contemplation, the answer became clear: The survivor's elation wasn't solely a result of his physical recovery; it was deeply rooted in his newfound awareness of life's unpredictability. Having stared into the abyss, he now viewed every heartbeat, every breath, as a precious gift. The very essence of life, once taken for granted, had been restored to its rightful place of reverence.

In contrast, the individual with a healthy heart—a truly fortunate state—had not come face to face with such a stark reminder of life's fleeting nature. With health as a constant companion, there was little impetus to actively acknowledge its presence. This phenomenon resonates with human nature: we often become so accustomed to abundance that we overlook its significance.

This encounter's lessons extend far beyond health. It's a mirror reflecting our tendency to overlook the beauty in the ordinary, the richness in the everyday. The relentless pursuit of success, material gain, and future aspirations blinds us to the beauty that graces our lives in the present. We're too busy charting our course to pause and recognize the splendor along the way.

Imagine a world where we pause to marvel at the hues of a sunset, find solace in a loved one's embrace, and derive joy from the simplest pleasures. By acknowledging that these moments are not guaranteed, that they could dissipate as swiftly as they materialized, our hearts would brim with gratitude.

In a landscape where life's blessings often blend into the background, let's strive to mirror the survivor's gratitude for the heartbeat that pulses within us. Let's embrace the notion that by acknowledging the impermanence of our blessings, we can infuse each day with a vibrant hue of gratitude. Through this lens, we can lead lives that are richer, more fulfilling, and infinitely more joyful.

In the culture we live in, where much is taken for granted, where life's melodies often fade into the background, let us tune our hearts to the rhythm of appreciation. Let's recognize that through conscious awareness, we can amplify our gratitude for the blessings that envelop us. By doing so, we awaken to a reality where every moment, every heartbeat, is an irreplaceable gift, deserving of our awe and heartfelt appreciation.

During a somber visit to an ailing friend, I was confronted with the stark reality of illness and vulnerability. As I stood by their bedside, accompanied by a friend who had joined me for the visit, an observation was shared that left me contemplating the delicate balance between modern medical advancements and the innate capabilities of the human body. My companion, gazing upon the intricate machinery that sustained our friend's fragile existence, remarked, "In the old days, there were no respirators. Someone in their condition would have likely succumbed to their ailment." I couldn't deny the accuracy of his statement; modern medical marvels like the respirator had indeed extended the boundaries of human survival. However, as I contemplated his words, a counterpoint emerged.

Turning to my friend, I offered a perspective that shifted the narrative: "You're absolutely right. In the past, such advanced medical interventions weren't available. But consider this: in those days, every individual possessed a remarkable gift—a built-in respirator." His quizzical expression prompted me to elaborate.

"The human body," I explained, "is an intricate masterpiece of God's design, equipped with an extraordinary ability to sustain life. Our lungs, our cardiovascular system—they function in perfect harmony, quietly ensuring our survival without requiring external assistance. The very breath that fills our lungs and sustains us is a testament to this innate capability."

To underscore the point, I invited my friend to step outside the realm of the hospital room and venture into the bustling corridors of the medical facility. There, amid the hum of machines and the scent of antiseptic, he would find individuals grappling with the harsh realities of illness and suffering. Their struggles would be palpable, their pain evident. This was the unadulterated reality of sickness, devoid of the comforts of modern medicine.

I urged him to take in the sight of the hospital beds, the strained expressions, the sound of labored breathing—all emblematic of the fragility of the human condition. Amid this poignant scene, the message was clear: our health, often taken for granted, was an irreplaceable gift.

By witnessing the suffering of others, we're offered a rare glimpse into the fragility of existence. The vitality that courses through our veins, the rhythm of our breath—these are the silent orchestrations of life itself. We often overlook these daily miracles until confronted with the stark reality of their absence.

As we walked out of the hospital, my friend's demeanor shifted. The gravity of the experience had left an impression, a reminder that our health is not a guaranteed constant. The built-in respirator that we all possess is an essential asset, an intricately woven thread that keeps the fabric of our lives intact.

It's human nature to be complacent about what we possess until we're confronted with the possibility of its absence. In a world where the miraculous has become ordinary, let's acknowledge the gift of each breath, each heartbeat. The next time we're tempted to take our health for granted, let's remember the hospital corridors, the struggles, and the silent resilience of those who long for the vitality we often overlook. Through this awareness, we can cultivate gratitude for the life-sustaining capabilities that reside within us, urging us to cherish the intricate symphony of our existence.

Make the Most of Your Circumstances

The story of an individual battling ALS left an indelible mark on my perspective, radiating a great sense of inspiration that continues to resonate within me. This individual was ensnared by the clutches of a debilitating illness, one that had ravaged his body to such an extent that his eyes were his sole functional conduits to the external world.

Unable to move or speak, he was imprisoned within the confines of his own physical limitations.

Yet, remarkably, he defied the odds by harnessing the one remaining element of agency—his eyes—to communicate and transcend his predicament. Employing an ingenious system that transformed eye movements into text on a computer screen, he managed to convey his thoughts and feelings letter by letter, word by word. His gaze, guided by an indomitable spirit, danced across the keyboard, constructing sentences and forging connections that defied the physical restraints of his body.

In the face of such adversity, many would have been consumed by a sense of grievance, bemoaning the unfair hand life had dealt them. But not this individual. Instead of fixating on the ravages of ALS, he directed his attention towards the one facet of his existence that remained intact—his eyes. These eyes, which shimmered with determination and resilience, became his lifeline to the world, serving as a testament to the boundless potential that resides within even the direst circumstances.

While it would have been easy to wallow in despair, he chose a different path—one of unwavering optimism and gratitude. He did not succumb to the weight of his misfortune; instead, he celebrated the marvel of his functioning eyes. With an attitude that defied the odds, he exuded a radiance of joy and contentment, unabated by the challenges that would have left many defeated.

He imparted a lesson that transcends the boundaries of his specific circumstances. His example underscores the power of perspective and the immeasurable value of focusing on what remains rather than dwelling on what is lost. While he could have bitterly lamented the myriad body parts that no longer responded to his will, he chose to revel in the vitality of his eyes, recognizing them as the conduits through which he could still express himself, connect with others, and be heard.

The juxtaposition between his circumstances and his attitude serves as a stark reminder of the boundless potential of the human spirit. Just as he found solace in his functioning eyes, we are compelled to acknowledge the countless blessings and abilities that we too often take for granted. Each breath we inhale, each step we take, every smile we share—these are not trivial occurrences but wondrous manifestations of our bodies' intricate symphony.

The story of this resilient individual serves as a catalyst for introspection, urging us to embrace gratitude for the simple yet profound elements that constitute our lives. By shifting our focus from perceived inadequacies to the strengths that persist, we can harness the transformative power of positivity, infusing each day with a newfound sense of purpose and joy.

In essence, his story unveils the art of finding light within the shadows, of embracing the fragments that remain whole amidst brokenness. Through his example, we are reminded that happiness need not be tethered to perfection. Even in the face of adversity, we can find reasons to celebrate, appreciate, and cherish. Just as his eyes became the source of his optimism, we can all discover our own sources of radiance, propelling us forward with a renewed zeal for life.

A humorous anecdote highlights the nature of perspective and the art of finding solace even in the face of challenges. In this tale, a person approaches his rabbi, weighed down by the burden of not having children. In his moment of vulnerability, he seeks empathy and understanding from the spiritual leader. The rabbi's response, however, takes an unexpected turn as he imparts a lesson about the relative nature of misfortune.

Upon hearing the man's lament, the rabbi begins his counsel by redirecting the individual's focus. The rabbi says to the man, "it could be worse." Puzzled, the man inquires about the hypothetical scenario that could surpass his current predicament of not having children. The rabbi's responds, "not having a wife is considered an even greater misfortune."

Undeterred, the man clarifies that he is also without a spouse. This prompts the rabbi to reiterate his point, suggesting that the situation could still be bleaker. Curiosity piqued, the individual queries how this could possibly be the case, given that he is devoid of both children and a spouse. The rabbi delivers the punchline, stating, "it could have happened to me"—a sentiment that wraps the tale into a comedic twist.

Beyond its humorous veneer, this tale delves into the essence of perspective and the intricate layers of human experience. The rabbi's responses, seemingly absurd at first, illustrate the way we work through our own troubles in relation to those of others. By demonstrating that another person could have faced the same challenges, the rabbi shifts the listener's perspective. This reframing of misfortune serves as a reminder that there are various facets to life's challenges and that we must always consider the broader context.

The story offers a subtle commentary on the tendency to focus on our own hardships without acknowledging the potential for greater struggles. It prompts us to reflect on the gifts we possess and the hurdles we have overcome, even as we acknowledge our struggles. Through humor, the story emphasizes the universality of human experiences, showcasing how we grapple with difficulties and the differing ways we respond to them.

At its core, the tale underscores the value of cultivating gratitude and the significance of recognizing the fortunes we often take for granted. It encourages us to recognize the silver linings within our own lives and to embrace the idea that, no matter our challenges, there are always alternate perspectives that offer fresh insights and a renewed sense of appreciation.

A fascinating anecdote from one of my followers highlights the intriguing ways in which our perspectives shape our experiences. This tale revolves around the act of generosity: adult children gifting a spacious home to elderly parents who were accustomed to residing in a small apartment. The children anticipated the joyful reactions of their parents as well as the future shared moments in the newfound space.

However, the outcome took an unexpected turn when the mother expressed her thoughts about the larger abode. Rather than rejoicing in the newfound comfort and potential for family gatherings, she articulated her concern about the increased distance she would need to walk within the expansive house. This seemingly trivial remark offers a powerful lesson in the art of perspective and the remarkable diversity in human thought.

The incident underscores that our perceptions are not solely influenced by external factors but are intrinsically shaped by the lens through which we view the world. In this case, the mother's focus was on the potential inconvenience of increased walking, overshadowing the benefits of the spacious dwelling. This story serves as a poignant reminder that even the most positive scenarios can be filtered through a negative lens if one's mindset is inclined toward skepticism or criticism.

The anecdote prompts us to reflect on our own reactions to life's offerings. How often do we find ourselves gravitating toward finding flaws, even when presented with something admirable? Conversely, have we encountered individuals who, regardless of their circumstances, radiate positivity and uncover silver linings? The story invites us to consider the impact of our perspective on our overall sense of contentment and appreciation. There are those who possess the remarkable ability to extract positivity from even the most challenging situations, while others may struggle to embrace the blessings bestowed upon them. This variance in perception extends beyond material possessions to encompass every facet of our lives.

Ultimately, the tale serves as a gentle reminder that our thoughts and attitudes wield significant influence over our interpretations. It encourages us to cultivate an awareness of our own predispositions and to consciously choose to adopt a more constructive outlook. By recognizing the potential for positivity even in the face of adversity, we can cultivate a mindset that empowers us to navigate life's complexities with resilience and grace.

I invite you to explore the depths of your own perspective and to embark on a journey of conscious introspection. Evaluate whether your interpretations are amplifying joy or magnifying negativity. By adopting a lens that seeks out the silver linings and cherishes the good, we have the opportunity to enrich our lives and elevate our experiences, ensuring that even the grandest of houses are appreciated for their inherent beauty rather than scrutinized for perceived inconveniences.

Don't Ignore or Be Overcome by Negative Experiences

In the realm of perspective, a simple yet insightful story emerges, shedding light on the different lenses through which individuals perceive the world around them. In a room where the chill was palpable, three distinct personalities illustrated the varied ways we engage with life's challenges.

Amidst the cold, the optimist emerged as a beacon of hope. With an unwavering faith in the sun's inevitable appearance, he projected a future of warmth and comfort. His optimism transcended the immediate discomfort, offering a reminder of the power of positive anticipation.

Contrastingly, the pessimist saw only the unyielding grasp of the cold. His perspective anchored in a sense of futility, he projected a perpetual chill that no external force could overcome. His viewpoint highlighted the potential pitfalls of dwelling in negativity, as it can color even the most hopeful situations with a sense of inevitable bleakness.

Amidst this interplay, the realist quietly intervened. Unperturbed by the extremes of optimism or pessimism, he focused on the practical. Recognizing the room's chill, he took action to address the situation, pragmatically turning on the heat to create a comfortable environment. His approach underscored the value of balanced and proactive responses to life's challenges.

Beyond this narrative lies a deeper truth—one that calls upon us to recognize the shades of goodness woven throughout existence.

Amidst the fluctuations of life's temperature, there is an innate inclination toward positivity. While challenges arise and circumstances
vary, the essence of life itself carries within it the potential for growth,
learning, and discovery.

In reality, the human experience encompasses both the warmth
of accomplishment and the chill of adversity. Just as the realist in
the story responded by adjusting the thermostat, we too possess the
agency to shape our lives through practical actions. While optimism
offers hope and pessimism demands caution, it is the realist's blend
of both, grounded in proactive steps, that often steers us toward the
most balanced path.

Ultimately, this story invites us to reflect on the way we perceive
life's challenges and joys. Just as the sun's warmth can break through
the chill of a room, so too can our positive outlook illuminate even
the darkest corners of our experiences. By embracing the lessons of the
optimist, the caution of the pessimist, and the practicality of the realist,
we craft a holistic view of life—one that embraces the full spectrum of
human emotions and seeks out the treasures of goodness that abound.
People often tell me that life is filled with tragedies; they suggest I look
at the news to witness heartbreaking stories. But in response, I ask
them to think about World War II. What were the headlines then?
Did they focus on those who survived or those who lost their lives?

This consideration shows something important: the news highlights only unusual events. In World War II, the focus was on survival
because, sadly, deaths were an everyday occurrence. This means that
if something's in the news, it's not a regular thing. So, when we see
sad stories on the news, it's a sign that these things aren't happening

all the time. The news picks out what's uncommon to share with us. In a way, it's a reminder that even though life has its share of tragedies, they're not the everyday norm.

CHAPTER 3

INNOVATE
TO SUCCEED

Challenge Perceived Limitations to
Unearth Your Creative Potential

Redefining success and embracing creative problem-solving are pivotal elements in unlocking your full potential in life. In a world marked by constant change and challenges, adhering to conventional definitions of success can be limiting and draining. By redefining success on personal terms, you can align your goals with authentic values and aspirations, cultivating a sense of fulfillment and purpose.

Innovation not only propels personal growth but also equips you to take on the complexities of life with resilience. It emphasizes the importance of continuous learning, resilience in the face of setbacks, and an openness to unconventional paths. Ultimately, by redefining success and embracing creative problem-solving, individuals pave the way for a more authentic and fulfilling journey, unleashing their untapped potential and contributing meaningfully to the world around them.

Set Realistic Self-Expectations

In the course of my interactions with diverse individuals, one individual's experience stands out—a person of immense talent who shared with me a perplexing sentiment. He confided that he often felt a sense of accomplishment inferior even to that of a homeless person. This enigmatic perspective was rooted in a strict correlation he had established between success and the attainment of 100 percent of his goals. If his achievements fell short of this flawless mark, regardless of the substantial progress he had made, he saw his efforts as futile. This dichotomy led him to expend exhaustive effort without reaping the rewards of self-recognition or tangible outcomes.

Intrigued by his perspective, I probed deeper, inquiring whether he could recall a single instance when he genuinely felt a sense of accomplishment. His response was unexpected. He struggled to remember any such moment. Expressing incredulity, I questioned whether, over the course of his life, he had truly never experienced a genuine feeling of accomplishment. Resolute in his stance, he maintained that this was indeed the case. I urged him to sift through his memories, guiding him toward an episode where he had executed a project that showcased his unique talents, leaving him with a genuine sense of fulfillment.

As he recounted this particular project, I gently posed a pivotal question: did he achieve 100 percent of his initially intended goal? His response held a valuable revelation; he acknowledged that he hadn't reached that elusive pinnacle but had instead realized approximately 85 percent of his target. I then probed further, drawing attention to his earlier assertion that any achievement shy of 100 percent was tantamount to failure. His response was enlightening: he recounted how, during this specific instance, his perspective had shifted. He found solace in the idea that, if a respected friend had accomplished the same 85 percent, he would view it as an impressive feat.

I seized upon this moment to underscore his innate capacity to devise coping mechanisms for his own benefit. Remarkably, without the aid of professional guidance, he had serendipitously unearthed a means to validate his accomplishments. I emphasized that this wisdom had originated within him and reminded him that he had effectively cracked the code to feeling proud of his achievements. In a curious twist, he had unknowingly discarded his own potent technique.

Drawing a parallel between the act of remembering and the process of studying, I underscored the notion that, just as one studies to retain knowledge, he needed to engage in a systematic study of recognizing his accomplishments. I encouraged him to incorporate this self-validation strategy into his routine consciously. Before starting any new project, I urged him to document his intention to counteract the tendency to belittle his accomplishments. This entailed embracing the perspective he would readily apply if his respected friend were beginning the same endeavor. By adopting this altered viewpoint, I believed he could nurture a more balanced appraisal of his own pursuits.

Driven by a desire to witness his personal growth, I offered a pragmatic approach, encouraging him to inscribe a simple statement before embarking on each project: "I am starting a new endeavor, fully aware of my predisposition to undermine my achievements and hastily label them as failures. To counteract this, I commit to viewing my efforts through the lens I would employ if my esteemed friend [mention friend's name] were taking on this very project." Guided by this counsel, he resolved to infuse this practice into his routine before tackling projects, from the momentous to the seemingly trivial. Astonishingly, he bore witness to a palpable elevation in his self-esteem, akin to the ascent of a resolute rocket ship piercing the heavens.

Here lies a remarkable technique, which could prove transformative when the weight of perfectionism leads you to believe that anything less than 100 percent attainment renders your efforts meaningless. Even if your goal didn't reach the full 100 percent mark from what you initially set out to achieve, I encourage you to reflect upon instances from your past when you experienced a genuine sense of accomplishment even when it did not reach your set-out goal in full. Hold onto these memories as a safeguard against falling into the trap of absolute perfection in your future endeavors. By doing so, you can liberate yourself from the shackles of unrealistic expectations and embrace the multifaceted nature of success.

Play to Your Strengths

A disillusioned salesman sought my advice, expressing his feelings of failure in the realm of sales. He contemplated leaving his job, convinced that success was eluding him. Intrigued by his predicament, I probed further, inquiring if he had achieved any sales at all. He admitted to a few promising deals but dismissed them as insufficient to sustain his livelihood. I pressed him for details on how he had clinched those particular successful deals. He divulged that his triumphs weren't anchored in his product pitch; rather, they emanated from building authentic connections with the owners. He revealed that he had effortlessly cultivated rapport, and a mutual fondness had blossomed between them. Moreover, he had offered heartfelt compliments that resonated with his genuine beliefs.

Recognizing the potential behind this approach, I suggested he encapsulate his method in a simple reminder by writing down: "I will foster connections with potential prospects akin to how I connected with [insert owner's name]." This step would serve as a compass, guiding him to consistently employ the strategies that had yielded success.

A few weeks later, the salesman returned with a renewed enthusiasm. He excitedly shared his transformative journey since our conversation. He marveled at the intricacies of the human mind, expressing wonder at how certain techniques can often lie dormant within us until awakened through self-awareness. He recounted that he had experienced remarkable success by revisiting his own innate abilities.

The realization dawned on him that he had inadvertently utilized these effective strategies previously but had allowed them to slip from his consciousness. Through mindful reflection and a renewed focus on his inherent strengths, he had tapped into his latent potential and rediscovered the tools that had always been at his disposal.

This story underscores the remarkable potential that exists within us, waiting to be rekindled by self-awareness and strategic mindfulness. Often, our own success lies hidden beneath layers of doubt and preconceived notions. The salesman's tale is a testament to the transformative power of acknowledging our strengths, even when they seem temporarily obscured. It's a reminder that success isn't solely about adopting new techniques but also about recognizing and revitalizing the strategies that have already proven effective.

In many aspects of life, we might overlook our innate capabilities in the pursuit of novelty. We chase after new methods and overlook the gems we already possess. This journey teaches us the importance of introspection, reflection, and understanding our unique strengths. By harnessing these tools and cultivating a mindset of self-confidence, we can unlock our full potential and pave the way for success.

The salesman's voyage of rediscovery teaches us that sometimes the most powerful solutions are the ones we've overlooked. Just as he reignited his career by tapping into his own proven strategies, we too can find success by acknowledging our strengths and embracing the unique qualities that set us apart. Success isn't always about reinventing the wheel; it's often about recognizing the wheel that's been there all along and learning how to steer it effectively.

Find Creative Solutions to Problems and Weaknesses

In the whimsical realm of sales, a tale unfolds that defies conventional expectations and adds a touch of humor to the art of persuasion. At the heart of this narrative lies a character whose stuttering speech seems to be in direct contradiction to his unparalleled success as a book salesman. As the tale goes, his triumphs on the sales floor surpass those of his fluent-tongued colleagues, leaving many curious minds to ponder the secret behind his unorthodox prowess.

It was within the bustling aisles of the bookstore that the protagonist's story took shape—a story blending audacity and wit in equal measure. His fellow colleagues, both eloquent and glib, found themselves in awe of his uncanny ability to clinch sales with a flourish, despite the rhythmic hurdles presented by his speech impediment.

Intrigued by this enigma, one of his peers finally decided to approach him and unveil the mystique that seemed to swirl around him.

"Pray tell," his colleague inquired, "how is it that you excel in this sales game with your unique challenge of stuttering? It defies the logic of our trade!" With a wry smile, the book salesman leaned in and offered a glimpse into his unassuming yet extremely effective strategy.

"I've found a simple approach," he began, "that cuts through the clutter and resonates with each individual I encounter. It's the embodiment of embracing my stutter as a unique advantage." His colleague leaned in, captivated by his words, eager to uncover the methodology that had sparked unparalleled success.

"Whenever I engage with a potential customer," he continued, "I don't let my speech impediment impede my intention. Instead, I present them with a choice that is both lighthearted and irresistible. I ask, 'Do you wish to purchase this book or shall I regale you with its contents?'"

A chuckle escaped his colleague's lips, recognizing the brilliance beneath the humor. "You mean to say," he laughed, "that you offer them the alternative of having you read the book aloud, as if it were an enticing performance?" The book salesman nodded, his eyes dancing with a playful gleam.

"Indeed! It's astonishing how this simple proposition breaks down barriers and transcends the initial awkwardness of my speech. By offering this alternative, I turn my potential challenge into an opportunity for amusement and engagement. It's as if they're invited to embark on a unique literary adventure with me as their guide. And more often than not, they choose the former—to purchase the book."

His colleague was struck by the ingenuity of the approach. "So, in essence, you've ingeniously transformed your speech challenge into a delightful interaction, a whimsical choice that beckons curiosity?"

"Exactly," the book salesman affirmed. "It's a testament to the fact that authenticity can disarm even the most guarded of souls. By acknowledging my stutter and weaving it into a narrative of choice, I create an atmosphere of genuine connection. The decision to buy becomes secondary to the camaraderie we share in that moment."

The tale of the stuttering book salesman serves as a reminder that the human spirit possesses an uncanny knack for turning limitations into avenues of creativity. It celebrates the idea that even in the face of challenges, the power of connection and authenticity can bridge gaps and triumph over obstacles. In a world where the pursuit of sales often seems dominated by eloquence and persuasion, this story stands as a whimsical testament to the enduring appeal of authenticity, humor, and the unanticipated strategies that lead to victory.

And so, in the realm of book sales, a stuttering salesman's unconventional approach left an indelible mark—a lesson that the heart's intent and the authenticity of connection can often outshine the most eloquent of pitches. The echoes of his proposition lingered, reminding us that even within the constraints of language, one can craft a symphony of engagement, bridging the gap between words and connection with a touch of wit and a dash of creativity.

In the face of challenges and limitations that may impede our progress, finding creative solutions becomes paramount for charting a path to success. Instead of allowing obstacles to be roadblocks, viewing them as opportunities to innovate and redefine our strategies can yield transformative results. Creative problem-solving enables us to transcend perceived limitations, turning them into steps toward success. By approaching challenges with a mindset that seeks innovative solutions, we not only overcome hurdles but also uncover hidden strengths and avenues for growth.

Go Where Others Won't

I want to share an observation that took root during my high school years. It dawned on me that individuals who possess extraordinary thinking capabilities sometimes grapple with lower self-esteem than their peers. This paradox may seem perplexing, but its origins lie in a fascinating dynamic. As deep thinkers immerse themselves in subjects with unparalleled thoroughness, they often find themselves outpacing their peers in understanding. However, this divergence can inadvertently lead to a skewed sense of self-worth.

Consider the scenario: a classroom where peers are skimming the surface of a topic, racing ahead in apparent swiftness. Meanwhile, the deep thinker delves into the intricacies, processing the information with meticulous depth. Amidst this, a notion takes root within the deep thinker—a notion that their pace is somehow slower than their peers, that they are lagging behind. Yet the truth often stands in stark contrast: these deep thinkers might be processing information at lightning speed, possessing an innate ability to swiftly work through difficulties. The disparity arises not from the speed of processing but from the sheer magnitude of knowledge they seek to assimilate.

An analogy comes to mind—a race between two individuals, John and Jimmy, scaling two different buildings. Picture this: John has soared to the thirtieth floor, while Jimmy has reached the fifth. Curiously, at this moment, Jimmy proclaims victory. Puzzled, we wonder,

how can Jimmy claim triumph when he's barely begun? The revelation
lies in the nature of the buildings they're ascending. Jimmy's structure is a modest five stories tall, while John's tower boasts a staggering
fifty floors. John has more to conquer, more distance to traverse. Yet
Jimmy's declaration holds a morsel of truth within its humor. This
illustrates a vital point: measuring success isn't solely about reaching
a predefined point but about recognizing the unique challenges and
contexts one faces.

This scenario mirrors a broader challenge in life—the uneven
playing fields we traverse. To bolster self-esteem, we must discard the
notion of comparison as a universal yardstick. A deep thinker's journey
isn't a simple parallel to their peers; it's a journey through dimensions
of understanding that others might not cover. Much like the varied
floors of John's and Jimmy's buildings, our paths differ. Elevating
self-esteem necessitates measuring against one's own playing field,
appreciating the nuances that define one's progress.

As we conclude this exploration, remember that the richness of
human experience lies not just in the destination but in the intricate
details of the journey. The deep thinkers among us possess a unique
perspective. It's a perspective that demands a distinct lens for assessment—one that recognizes the breadth and depth of knowledge
sought. So, let's cast aside comparisons and celebrate the unique
stories we each write within our distinct playing fields. After all, it's
not just the summit that matters but the wisdom gained and the path
taken to reach it.

In an intriguing encounter, an enterprising individual approached
me with an idea brimming with potential. Eager to share his vision, he

encountered a perplexing response: skepticism from those he discussed it with. This sentiment is all too common—the belief that if the idea were truly groundbreaking, someone would have already introduced it to the world. This is a sentiment that often echoes in the halls of innovation and invention. However, I shared with him a perspective that urged him not to be discouraged by such preconceptions.

I explained that throughout history, some of the most revolutionary concepts emerged precisely because they dared to challenge the status quo. The absence of a pre-existing solution does not automatically signal a lack of value in the idea. Rather, it could be the spark of something truly novel, waiting for someone with the vision to bring it to life.

To the individual who stood before me, I offered a counternarrative that carried a liberating message. Innovation frequently thrives in the spaces where individuals are willing to stray from the well-trodden path, daring to explore the uncharted territories of imagination. The concept that an idea must have precedents to be valuable is a misconception that has hindered countless creative minds.

I encouraged him to consider the irony of innovation: some of the most groundbreaking ideas arose precisely because someone dared to question the collective assumption that had stymied progress. In the realm of creativity, originality often springs from those who venture beyond the comfort of conformity.

Amidst the currents of conformity that often dominate our interactions, there exists an imperative to nurture independent thought and encourage creative exploration. Ideas that defy conventions might lack historical precedence, yet they hold the potential to redefine the landscape of innovation. The history of innovation is replete with stories of those who defied the notion that an idea must already exist to be valuable.

In the realm of innovation, it's often the audacious ideas that pave the way for transformative change. By challenging prevailing assumptions and embracing the calculated risks that come with breaking new ground, individuals can tap into potential waiting to be unlocked.

The unexplored path can be the one that holds the most promise. While the familiar might bring comfort, it's the uncharted territories of thought where genuine breakthroughs await. Don't underestimate the value of an idea simply because it hasn't been done before; instead, embrace the power of original thinking to shape the course of innovation.

Look for Answers from the Past

In the ever-evolving landscape of salesmanship, where connections and strategies are as pivotal as the products themselves, a seasoned salesman once unveiled a perplexing challenge that had tested the boundaries of his wit and resourcefulness. This particular roadblock involved the formidable task of establishing a direct line of communication with the CEO of a renowned corporation.

The salesman's preferred approach to navigating corporate hierarchy had been to build a relationship with a trusted assistant, strategically positioned in the proximity of the elusive CEO. This intermediary connection, he affirmed, was often the key to unlocking coveted meetings. However, this instance bucked the trend. Despite the assistant's diligent efforts and fervent pleas, the CEO remained resistant to their requests for a personal audience.

The question at the heart of our exploration was whether he had encountered a comparable challenge during his career. Initially hesitant, the salesman struggled to unearth such a memory. With gentle encouragement, I implored him to close his eyes and embark on a brief expedition into his past, granting his mind a mere five minutes to weave through the labyrinth of his experiences. To my astonishment, he resurfaced from this introspective journey with a tale that not only showcased his ingenious thinking but also encapsulated the enigmatic phenomenon of forgotten brilliance.

With a sense of anticipation, he began to unfold a story similar to the problem he was currently battling, "I once found myself teetering on the precipice of finalizing a monumental deal with a corporate giant. My connections seemed to be aligned, and my sales pitch was poised to seal the agreement. I could almost taste the triumph of success. Yet, as fate would have it, a seismic jolt awaited me. A call from a senior executive within the company informed me that the CEO had decisively rejected our proposal. The reasons behind this stunning about-face remained shrouded in mystery, leaving me baffled and disheartened."

As the story unfolded, a sliver of hope pierced the gloom: "Determined to turn the tide, I asked the executive for insights into how I might secure an audience with the CEO. My inquiry yielded a rather disheartening response. Meeting the CEO was nearly impossible. He had a steadfast resistance to discussing rejected proposals. The odds seemed insurmountable, to say the least. Yet I was determined to find a solution that could circumvent these seemingly impenetrable barriers."

It was at this juncture that his narrative assumed the stature of a testament to the limitless potential of human ingenuity: "As I wrestled with the challenge before me, a spark of inspiration ignited within. I once again reached out to the executive, humbly asking him to share the CEO's forthcoming flight itinerary—every detail from the departure time to the airline carrier. To my astonishment, my plea was met with a comprehensive dossier of travel particulars. I bought a business-class ticket for the very same flight."

The salesman's voice swelled with enthusiasm as he recounted the crescendo of his efforts: "As if choreographed by destiny itself, I found myself seated beside the CEO during the flight—an unprecedented stroke of fortune. The serendipitous encounter gave me a golden opportunity to initiate an authentic connection. In our conversation, I addressed his reservations about my proposal, peeling back the layers of his uncertainty to reveal the core of his objections. Furthermore, I presented a solution that resonated with his concerns, offering a conduit for alignment."

The salesman's words resonated with fervor as he unveiled the impact of this pivotal moment: "The exchange proved transformative—not only did I gain invaluable insights into his perspective, but I also garnered his support for our proposal. From that point onward, what had begun as a shattered dream evolved into an unparalleled triumph. The tide had turned, and the narrative was irreversibly rewritten."

Amidst the fervor of his storytelling, a revelation of significance emerged: "Upon reflecting on this chapter of my life, what struck me most was the connection between creative problem solving and memory. As someone who prides themselves on creativity, the very notion of momentarily forgetting a storyline of such magnitude was astonishing. Yet, upon introspection, I realized that the human experience is imbued with moments of transcendent inspiration, often mingling with the ebb and flow of daily life."

Empathizing with his experience, I offered my perspective: "This phenomenon is far from unique to your narrative. I've observed countless instances where individuals conceive ingenious solutions to challenges, only to watch those solutions elude their grasp in the passage of time. The interplay between memory and creative brilliance is both elusive and enchanting, a reminder that our minds are capable of conjuring ingenious ideas at the moments of their greatest need."

We explored the dimensions of memory and creativity, two forces intertwined in the journey toward success. This narrative illustrated that, even in the face of challenges and uncertainty, our minds possess the latent ability to unearth ingenious solutions.

Amid crafting this chapter, a memory from almost a decade ago resurfaced—a narrative showcasing the endurance of a property dispute worth tens of millions of dollars. The owner of the property had been locked in a relentless four-decade-long feud with an environmental group, resulting in an impasse that defied resolution.

I happened to know one of the owner's children, a philanthropic figure well known for his community contributions. Whenever I approached him with a request for financial aid to support individuals in need of mental assistance, his response was unfailingly positive. His generosity extended to significant financial contributions toward medical professionals caring for these individuals. During one conversation, he disclosed the exasperation his father felt due to the unrelenting feud with the environmental group. His father was earnestly seeking a resolution, yet the group's intransigence painted a grim picture for any potential breakthrough. In light of this, he turned to me with a plea for a creative strategy that might encourage dialogue with the group.

I agreed to contemplate this challenge, embarking on a quest to bridge the communication gap and cultivate a potential agreement. My initial outreach to the environmental group, however, met a frosty reception. They exhibited such deep-seated resentment toward the property owner that discussions appeared nearly impossible. Undeterred, I embarked on a brainstorming session, ransacking my memory for any comparable instances involving environmental groups or analogous scenarios. Regrettably, I couldn't summon any similar experiences from the depths of my recollection.

Months later, while scouring my files for a different document, I chanced upon an unexpected find—a document from years ago. Its contents left me incredulous. The document contained an agreement between a prominent real estate developer and, indeed, an environmental group. This artifact had been entrusted to me by the developer seven years prior, a testament to the trust he placed in our relationship. Little did I know, the document held the key to a long-forgotten tale of conflict resolution.

The real estate developer had shared this document with me years earlier, recounting how he applied his ingenuity to defuse a heated dispute on one of his properties. He narrated the story with a touch of pride, describing how his innovative approach had successfully breached the impasse. Two previously entrenched sides found common ground, and an equitable resolution was achieved.

This revelation struck me with awe—I had indeed forgotten a story of significance. The developer's technique, so perfectly tailored to the situation faced by my friend, remained latent in my memory.

In essence, it was the missing piece required to unlock a solution. Without further ado, I seized upon the technique and applied it to the ongoing four-decade-old feud. The results were astonishing, and the impasse finally dissolved, proving that even the most stubborn of conflicts can yield to a well-timed application of ingenuity and insight.

Our perceived limitations often act as invisible barriers that hinder our progress and creativity. When faced with challenges, there is a tendency to quickly succumb to the belief that certain obstacles are insurmountable. However, reflecting on past experiences in which we overcame setbacks can serve as a powerful antidote to this mindset. By revisiting moments when we defied odds and found creative solutions, we not only boost our confidence but also tap into a well of resilience and resourcefulness. These reflections can illuminate a path forward, providing valuable insights into our own capabilities and reminding us that creativity often flourishes in the face of adversity.

Moreover, the memories of overcoming challenges in the past hold untapped potential. They are not just reminders of our ability to overcome difficulties but also resources of innovative thinking and problem-solving strategies. Recalling instances where we navigated around roadblocks can spark creative insights, offering new perspectives on current challenges. By harnessing the lessons embedded in our past successes, we can break through the limitations we perceive, cultivating a mindset that propels us toward success and encourages the continuous cultivation of creativity in problem solving.

CHAPTER 4

TRUST YOUR INSTINCTS

Eliminate Indecisiveness by
Listening to Your Intuition

Indecisiveness has the potential to cast a shadow over our personal growth and leave us wandering in uncertainty about our identity and life's direction. This chapter delves into the transformative power of eliminating indecisiveness by tuning into our intuition. By emphasizing the importance of listening to our inner voice, we can learn to trust our instincts and make decisions aligned with our personal selves. As we uncover the role of intuition in dispelling confusion, we empower ourselves to approach crossroads with clarity, fostering not only better decision-making but also a more confident and purposeful existence.

It is only through making decisions and treading new paths that we will discover more of who we are and strengthen our values, beliefs, and goals. When we refuse to make decisions or if we let other people make the majority of our decisions for us, we risk becoming strangers to ourselves and getting lost on our way toward self-actualization and fulfillment.

Look to Past Triumphs

A person came to me with a complaint. He was struggling to make decisions, and his days were far from calm due to this constant uncertainty. I posed the question that I often do to those seeking guidance: "Can you recall a time when you were able to confidently make a final decision?"

Initially, he insisted that such a moment had never occurred, particularly not with significant decisions. "I wish I could give you just one example," he expressed, his frustration evident. After a lengthy conversation, he eventually managed to recollect a single instance where he did make a decision. I probed further, curious about his process. He shared that he had weighed all the pros and cons, assessing whether the benefits outweighed the drawbacks.

Intrigued, I questioned why he didn't apply the same approach to every decision. He responded that while the pros might indeed outweigh the cons in some cases, the cons still remained and couldn't be ignored. "Did the pros or cons disappear in that one decision you made?" I inquired. He admitted that they hadn't disappeared, but he realized that in life, the pros and cons rarely vanish completely. He understood that he simply needed to consider the overall balance, just as he had in that particular decision.

I pointed out that this mode of thinking was precisely what enables people to make decisions. I highlighted that he had inadvertently forgotten the approach he had successfully taken before, and now he was expecting the side that lost in the comparison to somehow disappear. I offered a suggestion: next time he's faced with a decision, he should, after listing the pros and cons, write at the top of the page: "I recognize that neither the pros nor the cons will vanish. However, as I did when I made that decision, I'll focus on what outweighs the other on the scale."

This simple reminder would serve as a compass, guiding him back to the effective mindset he once employed. Just as before, he could evaluate his options based on their overall weight and come to a decision with greater clarity.

I once met a man named Robert, a successful entrepreneur who seemed to have everything figured out. However, he had a secret struggle that often left him feeling overwhelmed: decision-making. Even the smallest choices, like what to have for breakfast, left him in a state of indecision.

One day, after spending hours agonizing over a seemingly insignificant choice, Robert decided he had had enough. He remembered a similar situation from his past when he successfully made a decision that had a positive outcome. It was a time when he was unsure about pursuing a new business venture. He had weighed the pros and cons, analyzed the risks, and ultimately took the leap. The venture turned out to be a great success.

Recalling this past experience sparked a realization in Robert. He recognized that he was capable of making decisions and that his method of evaluating pros and cons had served him well before. With renewed determination, he decided to approach decision-making in the same way.

The next time he faced a tough choice, Robert took out a piece of paper and listed the pros and cons. He reminded himself of the business venture he had once embarked upon and how his analysis had guided him to success. He wrote at the top of the page: "I have made good decisions before, and I can do it again."

As he compared the lists, Robert found that the clarity he sought began to emerge. He focused on what truly mattered—the overall impact and the potential outcomes. Armed with this mindset, he confidently made his choice.

To his amazement, the more he practiced this approach, the easier decision-making became. Over time, he realized that the key was not to eliminate doubts or fears but to acknowledge them and use his past successes as a reference point. Robert's ability to remind himself of his past triumphs in decision-making empowered him to overcome his struggles and lead his life with a newfound sense of confidence and clarity.

Rarely do we encounter choices with absolute clarity; doubts linger, and alternative paths haunt us. However, in navigating decisions, it's crucial to trust our instincts. Reflecting on past instances where we made decisions amid ambiguity and uncertainty can be enlightening. Many times, those decisions, though made with trepidation, proved to be the right ones in the long run. Embracing the reality that perfect clarity is elusive, we can draw strength from our own history of navigating the unknown. By acknowledging the doubts as inherent companions in decision-making and appreciating our ability to make sound choices despite them, we develop a mindset that empowers us to trust our instincts and confidently face the uncertainties of the future.

Consider the Long and Short-term Consequences

Deliberately considering both the long and short-term consequences and benefits of our decisions is an essential aspect of wise and strategic living. Short-term gains might offer immediate satisfaction, but a myopic focus on instant gratification can potentially lead to adverse long-term consequences. On the other hand, decisions informed by an understanding of their broader implications contribute to sustained well-being and future success.

By weighing the potential outcomes over different time frames, individuals make informed choices aligned with their overarching goals and values. This dual perspective promotes a holistic approach to decision-making, establishing a sense of responsibility and foresight. It underscores the notion that each decision serves as a building block shaping the trajectory of one's life. Striking a balance between short-term desires and long-term aspirations allows for a more intentional and fulfilling journey, where the choices made today resonate positively in the days, months, and years to come.

An easy way to implement this mindset is the famous 10-10-10 Rule. The 10-10-10 Rule is a powerful decision-making technique that helps you consider the potential consequences of your choices over different time frames: ten minutes, ten months, and ten years.

1. **10 Minutes:** Ask yourself, "How will I feel about this decision ten minutes from now?" This short-term perspective helps you gauge your immediate emotions and reactions to the choice.

2. **10 Months:** Next, consider, "How will I feel about this decision ten months from now?" This medium-term perspective encourages you to think about the effects of your choice on your goals, relationships, and commitments in the near future.

3. **10 Years:** Finally, contemplate, "How will I feel about this decision ten years from now?" This long-term perspective

prompts you to reflect on the potential consequences of your choice on your overall life direction, values, and aspirations.

By evaluating your decision from these three different time frames, you gain a more comprehensive understanding of its implications. It helps you avoid being swayed solely by short-term emotions or immediate gratification and instead guides you toward choices that align with your long-term goals and values.

The 10-10-10 Rule encourages you to consider the trade-offs, sacrifices, and benefits associated with your decision over time. It's a valuable tool to make more thoughtful and balanced choices that resonate with both your present and future selves.

Listen to Your Gut Instinct to Help Make Decisions

Caleb was notorious for being indecisive. He would spend hours agonizing over simple choices like what to eat for lunch or which movie to watch. One day, his friend Mike decided to help him overcome his decision-making paralysis.

"Caleb," Mike said, "I have a brilliant idea to help you make decisions more easily. We'll call it the 'Coin of Destiny.'"

Intrigued, Caleb asked, "What's the Coin of Destiny?"

"It's simple," Mike explained. "Whenever you're faced with a decision, you'll flip this special coin I've brought. If it lands heads, you'll choose the first option. If it's tails, you'll choose the second option."

Caleb chuckled, "Sounds like a fun game, but how will that actually help me?"

"Think about it," Mike said. "The moment that coin is in the air, you'll realize which outcome you're secretly hoping for. If you're disappointed with the coin's result, you'll know you wanted the other option all along."

Caleb agreed to give it a try. The next day, he faced his first decision: what to have for breakfast? He pulled out the Coin of Destiny and flipped it. It landed on heads, suggesting he should have cereal. However, as soon as he saw the result, he felt a pang of disappointment.

"You know what?" Caleb said with a grin, "I think I actually want potatoes and eggs."

Mike laughed, "See? The Coin of Destiny revealed your true desire."

Over time, Caleb continued to use the Coin of Destiny for decisions big and small. He found that the moment the coin was in the air, he would instinctively hope for a certain outcome. He realized that his hesitations and uncertainties were a sign of his true preferences.

Eventually, Caleb's decision-making skills improved. He learned to trust his instincts and make choices confidently. And while he still enjoyed the whimsical act of flipping the Coin of Destiny, he no longer needed it to guide his decisions.

So, Caleb's friends and family marveled at his newfound decisiveness, all thanks to a little coin that brought out his true desires and gave him the confidence to choose.

Making decisions is often a nuanced process, and our emotions can serve as valuable guides. Sometimes, committing to a decision and gauging our emotional response afterward can provide insights. The immediate emotional reaction can act as a compass, steering us toward understanding our true inclinations. If, in the aftermath, we sense a wave of disappointment, it may signal a misalignment with our desires, prompting a reconsideration or exploration of alternative choices. Conversely, a feeling of relief may signify that we've hit upon the right path. This practice of tuning into our emotions serves as a compass for both major life decisions and everyday choices, facilitating a more authentic and aligned approach to decision-making.

Realize a Decision Is Better than No Decision

There was once a renowned business coach who gave his friend a call and asked if he could borrow some money for a minor expense. The friend, a bit surprised, asked, "You're such a successful coach, why do you need to borrow money? Don't you have such a small amount on hand?"

The coach chuckled and said, "Well, you see, it's a bit complicated. I don't actually get paid."

Perplexed, the friend inquired, "Why not?"

The coach explained, "Whenever a client wants to pay for a coaching session and they ask me how much they owe, I always tell them that I'll get back to them with the answer."

The friend scratched his head. "So, they don't pay you because you don't give them a price right away?"

With a grin, the coach replied, "No, no, no! You've got it all wrong. I never actually get back to them."

Puzzled, the friend asked, "But why not?"

"Because," the coach said with a laugh, "I can't decide how much to charge per hour!"

The friend burst into laughter. "Oh, you're truly the brilliant coach, aren't you?"

As they both laughed heartily, the friend couldn't resist asking, "Anyway, how much money do you need?"

The coach's response was just as amusing, "To tell you the truth, I don't really know, because I can't decide about it."

The laughter between the two friends continued, almost causing them to fall on the floor.

Indecisiveness, if left unchecked, can obscure the path to personal growth and send us into a state of uncertainty. By attuning ourselves to the importance of listening to our inner voice, we learn to trust our instincts and make decisions aligned with our true selves. A decision, even if imperfect, is often better than the paralysis induced by indecision. As we face new decisions, let us embrace the wisdom gained in this chapter, empowering ourselves to make decisions with clarity, confidence, and a touch of humor.

CHAPTER 5

SUMMON YOUR RESILIENCE

*Overcome Resignation and Self-Pity to
Embrace Victory over Victimhood*

In the face of challenges, setbacks, or adversity, it's natural to experience moments of despair. However, true resilience lies in the ability to rise above these emotions, rejecting the role of a victim. Overcoming resignation and self-pity involves a conscious shift in mindset, acknowledging difficulties while actively seeking solutions. It entails a commitment to face adversity with courage, adaptability, and a belief in your capacity to overcome obstacles.

By cultivating resilience, individuals empower themselves to transform setbacks into opportunities for growth and triumph. Embracing victory over victimhood is not merely a triumph over external circumstances; it is an internal shift that propels individuals toward a future defined by strength, perseverance, and an unwavering belief in their ability to shape their future.

Harness Strength Despite Despair

During the tumultuous times of World War II, one story that inspires me is the remarkable uprising that took place in Sobibor. Amid the grim reality of death camps and the horrors of the Holocaust, the Sobibor uprising stands as a beacon of hope, showcasing the incredible strength of the human spirit and the power of a resolute can-do attitude.

In the somber expanse of death camps, where uprisings historically met with tragic defeat, the Sobibor uprising emerges as a rare and extraordinary triumph. This collective act of resistance, propelled by an unwavering determination to shatter the chains of oppression, stands as a testament to the indomitable human spirit prevailing against the darkest of circumstances. Unlike the majority of such endeavors, the inmates of Sobibor defied overwhelming odds, successfully toppling the oppressive SS staff that presided over the camp's horrors.

The narrative of the Sobibor uprising resonates as a powerful testimony to the enduring belief in the potential for change, even in the most despairing moments. In the face of the grim certainty of death, the prisoners clung steadfastly to the notion that, within the confines of the camp's walls, they retained agency over their minds and actions. This unwavering belief became the driving force behind their collective resolve to resist and fight for their lives against all odds.

The pivotal moment occurred on October 14, 1943, as members of the Sobibor underground orchestrated a clandestine operation resulting in the killing of eleven SS officers. Subsequently, around 300 prisoners were led to freedom—a remarkable achievement given the harrowing context of extermination camps. The backdrop to this uprising was the growing awareness among prisoners of Sobibor's imminent closure, which they understood would spell certain death, mirroring the fate of the last cohort of Bełżec prisoners. The Bełżec prisoners, forewarned by messages sewn into their clothing, communicated the ominous reality awaiting the Sobibor inmates: "Be aware that you will be killed also! Avenge us!"

An escape committee formed in response to these ominous rumors, led by Leon Feldhendler. Faced with betrayals and the constant threat of collective punishment, the committee navigated the delicate balance between secrecy and planning. However, by late September, progress had stalled due to their limited capacity to devise a strategic plan —none of the committee members possessed the military or strategic expertise necessary for a mass escape.

The turning point came on September 22, when approximately twenty Jewish Red Army POWs, including Alexander Pechersky, arrived at Sobibor. Pechersky, an actor, songwriter, and political commissar, would go on to play a central role in leading the revolt. The escape committee cautiously approached the newly arrived Russians, recognizing their military expertise as a potential asset. Pechersky, in particular, distinguished himself not only by standing up to SS officers but by exhibiting discretion in his defiance. Despite language barriers, Pechersky's commitment to the cause and his pragmatic approach impressed the committee.

Over the ensuing weeks, Pechersky met regularly with the escape committee in the women's barracks. Initial plans involving tunneling from the carpenter's workshop were deemed too challenging, prompting a shift in strategy. Pechersky's experiences in the forest brigade, where he heard a child's agonizing cries from the gas chamber "Mama!

Mama!," led to a profound realization: the plan could not merely facil-
itate an escape; it needed to foment a revolt. The ensuing weeks saw
the development of a comprehensive plan.

The uprising commenced in the late afternoon of October 14,
1943, unfolding in two phases. Covert killings of SS officers occurred
in the hour preceding the evening roll call, followed by a staged march
to freedom during roll call itself. The kapos would announce that the
SS had ordered a special work detail in the forest outside the camp,
and the entire group would calmly march to freedom out the front
gate. If the watchmen found this unusual, they would not be able to
confirm their suspicions or coordinate a response since the SS men
would be dead.

At 4:00 p.m., the Deputy Commandant of Sobibor, SS-Unter-
sturmführer Johann Niemann, arrived at the Lager I tailor's barracks
for an appointment with the head tailor. This rendezvous was orchestrated as a crucial moment for the conspirators, who aimed to prior-
itize Niemann's execution. The plan unfolded as Niemann was being
fitted for a jacket taken from a murdered Jew. The carefully orchestrated scene took a dramatic turn as Russian prisoners, armed with
axes, seized the moment and killed Niemann. They concealed his body
under a table, marking the beginning of a tumultuous hour. Over the
next sixty minutes, the camp witnessed a sequence of events that saw
one SS officer killed roughly every six minutes.

As the time for roll call approached, Alexander Pechersky, the
leader of the revolt, grew increasingly concerned about the potential
discovery of their plan. Despite the unexpected challenges, such as the
impulsive killing of Unterscharführer Walter Ryba, Pechersky hesitated to initiate the breakout prematurely, waiting for the opportune

moment linked to the demise of SS-Oberscharführer Karl Frenzel. Frenzel, known as one of the most dangerous officers in the camp, had delayed his arrival due to his time spent in the shower and his late appointment in the carpenter's shop. Finally, close to 5:00 pm, Pechersky and his associate Leitman decided to abandon their hope for Frenzel's participation in the plan and signaled the bugler Judah to climb the forester's tower and blow the bugle, announcing the end of the workday.

At this juncture, the Lager I prisoners had already left their jobs, congregating in the roll call yard or seeking refuge in nearby buildings. In Lager II, confusion reigned as prisoners, baffled by the early bugle call, gathered haphazardly for the march back to Lager I. Fearing that their disorderly lineup would attract the attention of the guards, Leon Feldhendler, a key figure in the revolt, took charge and led the march, singing the German tune "Es war ein Edelweiss." The atmosphere in the camp became tense as rumors about the revolt spread among the prisoners. A watchman's attempt to hasten the lineup led to an open altercation, with prisoners shouting, "Don't you know the war is over," resulting in the watchman's death. Realizing that the yard had become a potential powder keg, Pechersky intervened, delivering a speech to inform the prisoners of the unfolding revolt. The message emphasized the importance of facing their fate with honor and, if any survived, revealing the atrocities to the world.

As the prisoners dispersed, shots rang out from Lager II, fired by SS-Oberscharführer Erich Bauer. Bauer, returning from Chełm with a truck full of vodka, had ordered child prisoners to unload the cargo, leading to a tragic misunderstanding. Believing the children were responsible for the revolt, Bauer fired his pistol, killing one child and missing the other. The ensuing chaos saw prisoners running in all directions, killing a watchman and leaving many to make split-second decisions. The plan, kept on a need-to-know basis, left even those aware of the revolt with limited details. Pechersky and Feld-hendler attempted to shepherd prisoners to safety, but around 175 stayed behind.

The unfolding chaos led to a moment of confusion where the watchmen in the towers initially did not react. Some SS men hid, possibly thinking the camp was under attack by partisans. After a brief pause, the watchmen began shooting into the crowd. In response, some prisoners fired back using rifles obtained from Szmajzner, a prisoner in charge of the machine shop, and pistols taken from dead SS officers. A group of prisoners, positioned behind the carpenter's shop, used ladders, pliers, and axes left as a backup plan to scale the fence and traverse the ditch, running through the minefield toward the forest. This daring escape, however, was not without casualties, as exploding mines claimed some lives, drawing the attention of watch-men who intensified their gunfire.

Simultaneously, another group of prisoners headed for the Vorlager compound. Attempting to escape through the main gate or over the south fence, they encountered SS-Oberscharführer Karl Frenzel, who had emerged from the shower to get a pre-roll call drink. Frenzel, attracted by the commotion, armed himself with a machine gun and opened fire on the crowd. Pechersky, using SS-Scharführer Josef Vallaster's pistol, fired at Frenzel but missed. Some prisoners attempted to rush the main gate but were met by another SS officer, further intensifying the chaos. Despite the challenges, a significant number managed to trample the main gate and flood out.

In the Vorlager, prisoners sought alternative routes to escape, some attempting to climb over the barbed wire behind the SS officers' barracks, correctly assuming fewer mines in that area. However, many got entangled in the barbed wire. Thomas Blatt, among those stuck, survived as the fence collapsed on top of him. Witnessing the prisoners in front of him blown up by mines, Blatt freed himself by slipping out of his coat, stuck on the barbed wire, and ran across the exploded mines into the forest. Approximately 300 prisoners successfully escaped to the forest, marking a pivotal moment in the Sobibor uprising.[1]

The Sobibor uprising stands as a remarkable example of human resilience and the power of collective action. It highlights the potency of a can-do attitude in the face of overwhelming odds. The prisoners' unwavering belief in their capacity to bring about change, coupled with their strategic thinking and willingness to take risks, enabled them to achieve the impossible.

The legacy of the Sobibor uprising reminds us that even in the darkest of times, hope, determination, and strategic planning can lead to moments of triumph. It continues to inspire people to stand up against injustice, to unite for a common purpose, and to harness the strength within themselves to effect positive change, no matter how dire the circumstances may be.

Deep within each of us lies an inherent strength, an unyielding reservoir that becomes most apparent in the face of suffering and despair. It is a quiet force, often overlooked in the moments of calm, but when life's challenges surge, this internal fortitude emerges, resilient and steadfast. It is the source of courage that enables us to confront adversity head-on, the tenacity that propels us forward when the path seems bleak. Recognizing and harnessing this inner strength empowers us to endure, persevere, and emerge from the darkest tunnels of despair with newfound resilience and an unwavering belief in our capacity to overcome life's most formidable trials.

Find Connection When All Hope Seems Lost

In a quiet suburban neighborhood lived a mother named Emily and her adult son, Mark. Mark had always been a bright and talented individual, but as he entered his late teens and early twenties, he began to struggle with various challenges. He fell into a spiral of bad decisions, engaging in risky behaviors and distancing himself from his family.

As Mark's actions took him down a darker path, Emily found herself torn between frustration and worry. She saw her son making choices that hurt not only himself but also those who cared about him. However, Emily remembered the importance of unconditional love and acceptance that she had instilled in her children from a young age.

Rather than resorting to anger and judgment, Emily chose to reach out to Mark with an open heart. And she wrote him a very touching letter, which reads as follows:

Dear Mark,

I hope this letter finds you well. First and foremost, I want you to know how much I love you, unconditionally. No matter what path life has led you on, my feelings for you remain unwavering. As your mother, my heart is always open to you.

I've been doing a lot of thinking lately, reflecting on our journey together. Life has its ups and downs, and I know that sometimes the road can feel overwhelming. But I want you to understand that you're not alone in this. I am here for you, supporting you, and loving you every step of the way.

I remember the joy and happiness you brought into my life from the moment you were born. Your presence has always been a blessing, and it still is. I see the strength within you, the same strength that carried you through various phases of life. No matter what choices you've made, I believe in your ability to overcome any challenges that come your way.

I want you to know that my love for you is not tied to any expectations or conditions. It's not based on your achievements, successes, or even mistakes. My love for you is a deep, unwavering bond that transcends any circumstances. You are my child, and that alone makes you special and cherished.

Life is a journey of growth and learning, and sometimes we stumble along the way. But those stumbles do not define who you are. They are part of your story, just as much as your triumphs. I believe in your potential to find your way back to a path that brings you happiness and fulfillment.

Please remember that my door is always open, and my heart is always ready to listen. I want to understand your thoughts, your dreams, and your fears. Let's walk this journey together, just as we did when you were a child learning to take your first steps.

Mark, my hope for you is to find peace, happiness, and a sense of purpose. You have the power to create a positive change in your life, and I will be here to cheer you on every step of the way. You are loved beyond measure, and your well-being means the world to me.

With all my love and support,

Emily

Mark was very touched by the letter from his mother, and he wrote her back as follows:

Dear Mom,

Reading your letter brought a wave of emotions I thought I'd long buried. Your words struck a chord deep within me, reminding me of the warmth and connection we once shared. It's been a journey, one filled with highs and lows, but your willingness to reach out with an open heart has touched me in ways I can hardly express.

Life took unexpected turns for both of us, leading us down paths we never could have foreseen. The distance that grew between us wasn't easy for me either, and I've carried my share of regrets. Your honesty about your own struggles moved me, as it takes courage to lay our vulnerabilities bare.

I want you to know that your words have had a profound impact on me. The memories of our shared moments flooded back, reminding me of the bond we had and the person I used to be. Your acceptance and unwavering love despite everything I've been through mean more to me than I can convey.

As we take steps toward rebuilding what we once had, please know that I'm committed to making amends and rekindling our connection. I believe that the love and understanding we once shared can help guide us toward a brighter future. Your compassion has reminded me that there is goodness in this world, and I'm eager to embrace it once more.

Thank you for your letter, for your kindness, and for believing in the possibility of reconciliation. I look

forward to the journey ahead, as we walk this path
of healing and rediscovery together.

With heartfelt gratitude and love,

Mark

Over time, Emily continued to extend her love and support to
Mark even when he made mistakes or faced setbacks. She listened
without judgment when he shared his struggles and challenges, and
she offered guidance without forcing her opinions upon him. Emily's
unconditional acceptance created a safe space where Mark felt he
could open up about his struggles without fear of rejection.

Slowly but surely, Mark began to respond positively to his mother's approach. He felt the weight of his mistakes and the pressure to
live up to certain expectations gradually lift as he realized he was not
defined by his past choices. Emily's love and acceptance gave him the
strength to seek help, make amends, and work toward positive change.

As the years went by, Mark's journey toward recovery wasn't linear,
but Emily stood by his side throughout it all. Her unwavering love
and acceptance provided a foundation for him to rebuild his life. Mark
eventually found his way back to a healthier and happier path, realizing the value of his own potential and the importance of surrounding
himself with positive influences.

This story serves as a reminder that unconditional love and acceptance have the power to heal, inspire, and guide adult children even
when they've strayed from the right path. Emily's approach allowed

her to be a beacon of hope for her son, showing him that no matter how far he had wandered, there was always a place of love and acceptance waiting for him at home.

In the embrace of love and acceptance, we discover a healing force that transcends the wounds of disconnection. Love, in its many forms, possesses an inherent power to mend the fractures within our relationships and within ourselves. It is a resilient balm that soothes the pain of isolation and nourishes the roots of connection. When we offer and receive love authentically, it becomes a catalyst for transformation, cultivating a resilience that allows relationships to weather the storms of life.

Don't Let Roadblocks Stop Your Progress

The journey of individuals grappling with obsessive-compulsive disorder (OCD) is marked by profound challenges. Beyond the persistent doubts that erode tranquility, a more insidious belief often takes root for those who suffer from OCD—that something is inherently awry within themselves. This perception can unleash a cascading decline in self-esteem, affecting every facet of their lives. Within this chapter, we will delve deeper into this struggle, aiming to shed light on an inspiring fact: many of those enduring this ordeal are exceptionally talented individuals. By recounting the stories of these gifted individuals who have battled OCD firsthand, I aim to showcase that hidden within the struggle is the potential for greatness and self-worth restoration.

I once met a person who faced significant challenges due to OCD. Beyond the difficulties caused by the disorder itself, he also struggled with feelings of worthlessness and a sense that something was wrong with him. Before delving into strategies to address OCD, I wanted to address the core pain he experienced: the feeling that he didn't measure up. I asked him if there were times when he accepted his OCD and didn't judge himself harshly. However, he couldn't recall such moments. I encouraged him to think about others he might know who also had OCD. After some thought, he remembered a few individuals who had dealt with the disorder to varying degrees.

Continuing our conversation, I inquired whether any of these individuals he knew were admirable to him. He revealed that one person he admired had a successful business and displayed remarkable creativity in attracting significant clients. It was only when he saw this person at gatherings that his self-doubt seemed to quiet down. Recognizing that even talented people struggled with OCD helped alleviate his feelings of inadequacy. I pointed out that he had already managed to find solace in this realization on occasion, without consciously remembering it.

I suggested he start writing down the following affirmation daily: "I acknowledge that individuals with OCD possess talents that are anything but average. In fact, they might possess above-average talents. For instance, I've observed [write in name] who grapples with OCD yet achieves remarkable success. Therefore, I will not belittle myself or measure my self-worth due to this disorder." I advised him to write this affirmation daily until it became ingrained in his mindset.

He followed through on this practice and, after some time, reported a significant improvement in his perception of his self-worth. With that foundation in place, we began addressing the OCD itself. I presented to him a collection of illustrious and gifted historical figures whose lives were colored by the shades of OCD. Through their experiences, I hoped to draw parallels and inspire this individual to recognize their potential for overcoming adversity.

One such luminary was Nikola Tesla, born on July 10, 1856, in Smiljan, Croatia, then part of the Austrian Empire. From his early years, Tesla demonstrated a remarkable aptitude for engineering and invention. His journey led him to study electrical engineering at the Austrian Polytechnic University in Graz and later at the Charles-Ferdinand University in Prague. These foundational experiences paved the way for his subsequent work with telegraph and electrical companies across Europe.

However, the turning point in Tesla's life came in 1884 when he emigrated to the United States. He embarked on a collaborative journey with Thomas Edison, albeit short-lived due to differing views on electrical systems—Edison championing direct current (DC) while Tesla vouched for alternating current (AC). In a defining partnership with George Westinghouse, Tesla championed AC power transmission, revolutionizing modern electrical distribution systems.[2]

Tesla was a prolific inventor, with his inventive portfolio encompassing groundbreaking technologies such as the Tesla coil, alternating current motors, and the radical concept of wireless transmission of electricity. His ingenious mind resulted in approximately 300 patents by the time of his demise. Beyond his scientific contributions, Tesla's legacy is woven into the fabric of modern electrical systems and technology. His ideas have served as the foundation for subsequent innovations, continuously inspiring scientists, engineers, and inventors.[3]

Nikola Tesla's life is often examined for signs of obsessive-compulsive disorder (OCD). Reports suggest that Tesla exhibited a range of behaviors that align with OCD tendencies.

- One manifestation was Tesla's fascination with numbers, particularly the number three. He reportedly engaged in rituals that revolved around the number three, such as pacing around a building three times before entering. This behavior resonates with the need for symmetry and precision often observed in individuals with OCD.
- Tesla's meticulousness extended to everyday actions, such as his need for precisely eighteen napkins to clean his utensils during meals, highlighting an inclination toward repetitive and ritualistic behavior, a characteristic of OCD.
- Hygiene and cleanliness concerns are another hallmark of OCD, and Tesla demonstrated a pronounced aversion to germs and dirt. He often shied away from shaking hands with others due to a fear of contamination.[4]

Even some of the most accomplished people face internal struggles that most people aren't aware of. We all have human traits, whether mental disorders, chronic illness, or behavioral issues, that could become devastating roadblocks to our potential if we allow them. But if we arm ourselves with the resilience necessary to take on whatever life throws our way, then those things that may have once been roadblocks will become tangential parts of our stories.

Let Your Unique Identity Guide Your Path Forward

I had the privilege of engaging in a deeply enlightening conversation with a Holocaust survivor whose innate positivity and resolute attitude illuminated the darkest corners of his experiences. In my quest to understand his journey of survival, he shared a remarkable anecdote that beautifully exemplifies the influence of positive thinking and a determined mindset.

Joseph's story unfolded against the backdrop of a war-torn world, a place where human compassion was scarce and survival was a constant struggle. He was a mere twenty years old as the war neared its gruesome end. The Nazis, masters of cruelty and torment, forced him into a relentless death march, a chilling procession where participants dragged themselves forward, weighed down by burdens of heavy concrete. The goal was to march until one's strength faltered, and death inevitably ensued. Joseph found himself under the watchful eye of a lone Ukrainian guard, armed and ready to enforce the Nazis' inhumane orders.

Faced with the dire predicament before him, Joseph's mind became a battleground of thoughts. A determined thinker with a penchant for innovation, he began devising a plan to extricate himself from the clutches of this harrowing ordeal. He found solace in the approaching Jewish Sabbath, a time of spiritual reflection and observance. Inspired by the thought, Joseph formulated an audacious strategy that showcased the power of positive thinking and resourcefulness.

Joseph approached the guard with an unusual request, one that defied the cruel reality of their circumstances. He asked if he and his friend could engage in song to honor the holy day. To his astonishment, the guard consented. As the Sabbath sun dipped below the horizon, Joseph and his friend embarked on a hauntingly beautiful

Hebrew melody, their voices harmonizing in a poignant tribute to tradition. Yet beneath the lyrics lay a clandestine dialogue, a discourse fueled by hope and the desire for liberation.

Joseph's storytelling voice took on a more animated tone as he recounted the events that followed. He relayed how he and his friend utilized the cover of the song to exchange thoughts, ideas, and strategies for escape. By ingeniously blending their animated conversation with the song's rhythm, they managed to forge a plan in the midst of their captor's unsuspecting gaze. This ingenious blending of song and dialogue would later become a hallmark of Joseph's tenacity and resolve.

Joseph shifted back to his own voice, recounting the tense atmosphere that hung in the air as he and his friend continued their covert conversation. He smiled as he recalled how he encouraged his friend to contribute his own thoughts while maintaining the façade of a spirited performance. This ingenious ruse enabled them to discuss their strategy while sidestepping the scrutiny of the watchful guard.

With a twinkle in his eye, Joseph resumed his storytelling voice to recount the pivotal moment that followed. Their animated conversation seamlessly transitioned into a resounding declaration of unity and purpose. Joseph suggested they synchronize their efforts and, on the count of three, hurl the massive blocks of concrete at the guard, incapacitating him and seizing their chance for freedom. His friend eagerly embraced the plan, the embodiment of Joseph's unwavering positivity and resourcefulness.

The story unfolded with breathless anticipation as Joseph recounted the heart-pounding moment of truth. On the count of three, their synchronized efforts were set in motion, and the heavy concrete found its mark. The guard crumbled to the ground, dazed and incapacitated by the unexpected assault. In that critical moment, Joseph and his friend seized their chance and fled into the night, leaving behind the bonds of captivity.

Joseph's tale is a testament to the resolute power of the human spirit and the transformative potential of positive thinking. Through sheer determination and unwavering optimism, he managed to defy the odds and engineer his own liberation. His story serves as a poignant reminder that even in the bleakest of circumstances, a positive mindset and an indomitable can-do attitude can ignite the spark of hope and pave the way to survival.

As our conversation drew to a close, I expressed my heartfelt gratitude to Joseph for sharing his story. His narrative underscores the importance of positivity and resilience in the face of adversity. His ability to navigate the most harrowing circumstances with a spirit of innovation and hope stands as a beacon of inspiration for us all. Joseph's legacy serves as a testament to the unwavering human capacity to triumph over darkness and emerge victorious through the transformative power of resilience.

In a world that is all too often consumed by comparison and self-centeredness, this story serves as a gentle nudge toward a more expansive outlook. It invites us to chuckle at life's ironies, embrace the wisdom of perspective, and find humor in our individual journeys.

While the daily challenges of your life may not be as bleak as those who were subjected to death camps, I hope you've found seeds of hope in this chapter that will grow to become a resilience to take on all life throws your way. We don't always get to choose what happens to us in this life, but we do choose how we respond. When we respond to life's trials with resilience, we find the necessary strength, hope, and connection that helps us through the darkness of despair into the light of growth and achievement.

CHAPTER 6
EMBRACE CHANGE

Face the Unknown with Hope

Through navigating the ebbs and flows of life, we learn, grow, and develop into the individuals we were born to become. Resisting change can lead to stagnation, whereas embracing it opens doors to new possibilities, promoting a sense of flexibility and an enriched perspective on the world around us. Change challenges our resilience, broadens our perspectives, and encourages us to step outside our comfort zones. Rather than resisting the inevitable shifts that life presents, welcoming change with open arms enables us to harness its transformative power. Embracing change is not merely a passive acceptance; it is an active engagement with the dynamic nature of existence. When faced with the unknown, approaching life with hope and self-assurance becomes a guiding light.

Life's fluctuations challenge us to reevaluate our goals, reconsider our priorities, and tap into strength we may not have known existed. With an open heart and an optimistic outlook, we can approach change as an ally, recognizing that in its currents lies the potential for self-discovery, resilience, and a great sense of fulfillment in the ongoing journey of becoming our truest selves.

Recollect the Positives of Change

As I strolled through a bustling park one sunny afternoon, I noticed a young man sitting on a bench, his demeanor a stark contrast to the vibrant surroundings. He appeared visibly nervous, his brows furrowed, and his fingers fidgeting restlessly.

Intrigued by his troubled expression, I approached him, introducing myself. He introduced himself as Jake, a soon-to-be groom. Jake seemed caught in a whirlwind of anxiety, and he couldn't understand why. He asked me with a hint of desperation, "Why am I feeling so nervous when I should be over the moon about my upcoming wedding?"

I took a moment to ponder his question and soon realized that his apprehension might be rooted in the age-old fear of the unknown. The unknown, in this case, was the uncertainty of how his marriage might unfold. He nodded slowly, a glimmer of recognition in his eyes.

"What can I do about it?" he implored, his voice tinged with desperation.

My response was far from a simple platitude. I shared with Jake a technique that has often proven invaluable in times of anxiety and change: the power of recollection. I urged him to journey back into his past, to pinpoint a moment when a significant change had loomed on his horizon. A sense of fear and uncertainty had gripped him then, much like the present moment.

Jake's memory led him to a time when he had embarked on a new job in a different city. The mere thought of it had consumed him with anxiety, casting a long shadow of uncertainty over his path. But, as he reflected on it, he realized that he had not only survived that transition but had thrived in his new life.

I encouraged him to delve further, to explore the details of what had calmed him down during that challenging period. He explained how he had found solace by recalling other instances when he had faced the abyss of the unknown. As he recounted stories of past changes, he saw a common thread: he had consistently emerged stronger and more resilient from each transition.

"You see, Jake," I pointed out, "you already possess a powerful tool to find your way through this emotional storm. By reminding yourself of those past experiences of change that you initially feared but which ultimately worked out, you can find comfort in your innate ability to adapt."

Jake's eyes widened, as if a veil had been lifted from his understanding. This self-comforting mechanism had always been within him, but he had never consciously recognized it. It was as if he had found an anchor to steady himself amidst the turbulent sea of change.

Fueled by this newfound insight, Jake decided to take action. With a pen in hand, he began to write down each past experience of change that had initially caused him anxiety but had, in the end, unraveled positively. The process was therapeutic, soothing his racing thoughts and reinforcing his resilience.

But there was one more piece to this puzzle of managing change. I asked Jake to confront the lurking monsters of his subconscious— the worst-case scenarios he was envisioning. These fears, I explained, often dwell beneath the surface, making them harder to confront. But by giving them a tangible form through writing, his conscious mind would become more aware of these anxious thoughts, paving the way for effective management and, ultimately, their defeat.

As Jake filled the pages with his deepest fears, I could see a transformation occurring before my eyes. The lines on his face seemed to soften, and the tension in his shoulders gradually melted away. He had, in this journey of self-discovery, found the tools he needed to confront his fears head-on.

With newfound clarity and a sense of empowerment, Jake left the park that day with a renewed spirit. He realized that the key to handling change lay not only in acknowledging the fear of the unknown but also in embracing the strength that comes from facing it. The wedding preparations resumed, but this time he faced them with a calm and confident demeanor, ready to embark on his new life with resilience and optimism.

I came to understand that the reason why God instilled inherent fear of change in us is that if change were effortless, there would be little stability in the world. People might switch homes, partners, and vehicles so frequently that it would disrupt the fundamental stability of our lives. Thus, it appears that this resistance to change is a mechanism designed to ensure that we only make significant changes when they are truly necessary.

Prepare Yourself for Significant Changes

Once, in a small coastal town, there lived a seasoned sailor named Captain Morgan. He was known for his adventurous spirit and the ability to navigate through life's storms. One day, a sudden and unexpected hurricane was predicted to sweep through the town, leaving chaos in its wake.

While others were scrambling to secure their belongings, Captain Morgan calmly gathered his crew and prepared his ship, "The Resilience." He had spent years honing his sailing skills and knew that change, much like the unpredictable sea, was inevitable.

As the storm intensified, Captain Morgan skillfully adjusted the sails, tightened the rigging, and ensured every crew member was equipped with a life jacket. His ship, well-maintained and sturdy, stood resilient against the fury of the storm. Amid the howling winds and crashing waves, Captain Morgan's calm demeanor and meticulous preparation inspired his crew. He demonstrated the importance of adaptability and being ready for the unexpected twists of life.

When the storm finally passed, the town faced the aftermath. Many had suffered losses, but Captain Morgan and his crew emerged unscathed. Their preparedness and ability to navigate through the turbulent times became a legend in the town, teaching everyone the invaluable lesson that, in the face of change, preparation and resilience are the anchors that keep us steady.

When we accept the inevitability of change, prepare for it, and face it with resilience, we are able to face the storms of life and the winds of change knowing that we will make it through and learn an important lesson in the process.

Different Circumstances, Same Team

People are ever-evolving and so are the circumstances of life, which often means relationships change throughout the course of life. Marriages often begin during periods of differing success levels, and situations can evolve when one spouse experiences a surge in accomplishment, perhaps in business or other endeavors. Amidst this transformation, an individual with low self-esteem might wrestle with insecurities, fearing that their partner's newfound success could lead to abandonment. To mitigate this concern, it is imperative for the accomplished spouse to actively communicate that their achievements are a shared victory.

This is not merely a reassurance but a commitment to unity and mutual growth. By firmly emphasizing that both partners are a team, and that one person's success directly enhances the quality of life for both, potential conflicts rooted in misperceptions can be averted. This approach not only fortifies the bond between spouses but also reinforces the understanding that love and support are unwavering regardless of individual achievements.

Change is inevitable, and within the shifting dynamics, the strength of our connections lie in the understanding that we face these transformations hand in hand. Recognizing that challenges and shifts are shared experiences allows for a cooperative approach, reinforcing the notion that, as a team, we can overcome any obstacle or welcome any evolution that life presents. Embracing change within the context of unity deepens the bonds that tie us together, ensuring that the journey, with all its twists and turns, is faced with shared resolve.

Embracing change is more than adapting to the circumstances that life throws at us; it's an active participation in our own growth and transformation. The importance lies not just in accommodating external shifts but in allowing these experiences to be catalysts for internal evolution. Life's surprises and challenges provide an ever-changing opportunity to develop our character. It's not merely about letting the circumstances dictate who we become but rather about the conscious, introspective response we choose to craft in the face of change.

In this nuanced dance with life, we find the power to shape our character through intentional reflection and thoughtful adaptation. By embracing change with a mindset of active participation, we ensure that we are not molded by external forces alone. Instead, we become the architects of our own growth, sculpting resilience, wisdom, and depth through each encounter with life's inevitable shifts. This approach helps us better embrace change, transforming what could be perceived as disruptions into opportunities for self-discovery and the continual refinement of our authentic selves.

PART 2

MASTER
YOUR
EMOTIONS

CHAPTER 7

ARM YOURSELF WITH INFORMATION

*Quell Your Fears by Gaining
Knowledge and Perspective*

Think of the fears you had as a child. Maybe you were afraid of the dark, terrified of monsters under your bed, or deeply startled by loud noises. As we grow up and experience more life and accrue more knowledge, these childhood fears tend to dissipate.

It's not that fear in itself disappears entirely; instead, our fears from childhood are often replaced by adult fears that delve into the realms of personal health, finances, tragedy, and death. Sometimes, even when the probability of our fears materializing is incredibly low, we are unable to shake the fear entirely. This chapter explores the ins and outs of our fears, rational and irrational, and offers practices that can help you mitigate fear and live fully.

Realize the Power of Your Imagination

People are often overwhelmed by fear, whether it pertains to their health or external circumstances. I recall an instance where an individual expressed a deep concern that he might be suffering from cancer, fearing the worst. Curious, I inquired, "What leads you to believe that you are afflicted with such a grave illness? To me, you appear to be in perfect health. Can you describe the symptoms you're experiencing?" With a trembling voice and hands, he pointed to the left side of his head, indicating the precise spot of his discomfort.

In response, I suggested, "If the pain you're feeling is concentrated there, it could be related to diabetes." Taken aback, he asked, "Why diabetes? How can you possibly know? Are you a doctor?" To this, I countered, "How do you know it's cancer? Are you a doctor?" He chuckled and then admitted I had a point. He acknowledged that by day's end, he recognizes that he lacks the expertise to diagnose himself and that the symptoms he experiences might not be as dire as he fears.

I encouraged him to seek resolution rather than dwell in worry. "Why not consult a doctor to ascertain the cause of the pain?" I proposed. This person, you see, discovered for himself a means to alleviate his apprehensions. Yet, he encountered difficulty in retaining this calming perspective. He kept forgetting his own reassuring thoughts, leaving him susceptible to recurring fears. In response, I suggested that he document these thoughts to prevent their loss when faced with future anxieties.

He then asked me why people tend to jump to conclusions in areas where they lack any knowledge. I explained that this is a common trait of human nature. When individuals lack certain information, they often fill in the gaps with their own imagination. For instance, think about when you talk to a stranger on the phone, you immediately conjure up an image of how that person looks, even though you have no actual basis for it. It's fascinating how far our imagination can be from reality when we eventually meet that person.

When you're grappling with fear, whether it's related to your health or external events like accidents, it's essential to recall instances when you weren't as afraid of those thoughts. Take the time to identify the counteractive thoughts that brought you comfort, even if you've forgotten them. Then make it a mission to jot them down and remember them consistently, not just occasionally. This practice can help you reclaim a sense of calm and resilience.

When it comes to fears, I've noticed something interesting. People tend to fear things that have a very slim chance of actually happening, just because there's a possibility. But there are many other things in their daily lives that have a much higher chance of going wrong or causing harm, yet they're not afraid of those. They'll even say, "Oh, the chances of that happening are so low, I'm not worried." For instance, someone might fear their house catching fire in the middle of the night, but they won't be afraid of a car accident even though statistically, it's more likely. This same mindset applies to different situations. And here's an interesting point: people won't throw a party to celebrate if they buy a lottery ticket and have a chance to win.

Once, a friend confided in me about his fear of being targeted on the street and shot. This fear consumed him no matter where he was, causing him to vividly imagine the sensation of bullets piercing his body and gradually feeling his strength wane. In an attempt to help him rationalize, I pointed out the power of imagination in intensifying these feelings. I explained that he was essentially envisioning himself being shot, already sensing the bullets and even imagining a weakening sensation. However, I countered his belief by sharing the reality that if he were genuinely shot, he wouldn't experience a gradual loss of strength. In fact, the immediate impact of a gunshot wound would likely render him unconscious and lying on the ground rather than experiencing a gradual decline.

This interaction exemplified how our imagination can magnify our fears beyond the bounds of reality. The mind can concoct elaborate scenarios that intensify our anxieties, leading us down a rabbit hole of unfounded worry. Recognizing the stark contrast between our imagined fears and the actual outcomes can help put our worries into perspective. Understanding that our minds can create scenarios far more dramatic than reality can serve as a powerful tool in managing and eventually overcoming these paralyzing fears.

I've come to realize that many life problems tend to resurface repeatedly throughout a person's journey. Fears, in particular, follow this pattern. How often do we experience specific symptoms, triggering a fear of a serious ailment? It's intriguing how, even after consulting a doctor in the past for similar symptoms, which turned out to be nothing of concern, we still fall into the same anxiety when those symptoms recur. This recurrence highlights the power of our imagination and our predisposition to worry. It's a reminder that our minds can magnify possibilities, leading us down unnecessary paths of fear, even when past experiences should offer reassurance.

We've previously discussed how fear can stem from misinformation combined with imaginative thoughts detached from reality. The mind, lacking accurate information, often fills gaps with unsubstantiated ideas, causing the imagination to run wild.

I once had a conversation with a well-known and respected

medical doctor who had treated countless patients over the years. It was about the delicate matter of addressing people's health fears. I shared with him my observations that simply assuring individuals that everything appeared fine, and there were no apparent signs of illness, didn't always provide the comfort needed. Not everyone would instantly calm down or stop obsessing over their fears, even if all the medical tests came back normal.

I highlighted the complexity of this issue, particularly for those grappling with severe health fears. These individuals aren't content with a superficial assurance; they yearn to understand the underlying causes of their physical sensations and symptoms. They're plagued by questions like, "Why do I feel this pain in my body?" It's this desire for clarity that often sends them on a relentless quest for answers.

In my conversation with the doctor, I stressed the importance of transparency. I suggested that it's crucial to share the truth with these patients. There's a wealth of scientific research illustrating that stress, in and of itself, can trigger a wide array of physical discomforts. It's not uncommon for stress to manifest as various types of pain, even if no serious medical condition is present.

Imagine someone experiencing an unfamiliar pain. Their immediate reaction is to worry about what might be causing it. In the case of those with heightened health fears, the concern can escalate into an overpowering fear that a grave illness is at play. The emotional stress compounds the physical sensations, intensifying the pain and discomfort. It's a vicious cycle, a Catch-22: the stress about the unknown in the body causing physical pain, and the pain in turn increasing the fear and anxiety.

I explained to the doctor that failing to address this dynamic could exacerbate the situation. Without an explanation, patients might begin doubting the accuracy of medical tests. They might think that the tests somehow missed a hidden illness. The lack of information could trigger further stress and heighten their fear, perpetuating the cycle of physical discomfort and emotional distress.

This doctor, who had seen a plethora of medical cases throughout his career, understood the significance of addressing not just the physical symptoms but also the emotional concerns. He agreed that offering patients a well-rounded explanation, grounded in scientific understanding, could go a long way in helping them manage their fears. We discussed the potential of creating a more holistic approach to medical consultations, one that includes discussions about the mind-body connection and the powerful influence of stress on physical well-being.

In the end, our conversation emphasized the importance of open communication, education, and empathy when dealing with individuals plagued by health fears. A comprehensive approach that integrates medical knowledge with psychological insights could potentially provide much-needed relief and empowerment to those struggling with the overwhelming burden of fear and uncertainty.

Acknowledge the Sway of Influence

Imagine a group of friends who conspired to play a prank on their unsuspecting companion. This individual, let's call him Ben, stepped out of his home one morning, unaware of the events that would soon unfold. As he walked along his usual route, he encountered a friend at the first corner. This friend commented on Ben's pallid complexion, expressing concern for his well-being. Bewildered, Ben dismissed the comment, attributing his appearance to mere happenstance.

Continuing his journey, Ben arrived at the second corner, only to encounter another friend. This friend, too, noticed his unsettling appearance, expressing worry over his condition. Ben's reassurances became less convincing, his unease growing. Puzzled and slightly distressed, he carried on, reaching the third corner where yet another friend awaited.

This time, the friend's observation was more dire. He reported that Ben seemed on the verge of collapsing. Panicked and feeling the weight of his friends' remarks, Ben's anxiety escalated. His breathing grew labored; his feet began to tremble, and a sense of weakness consumed him. Despite his attempt to remain composed, he couldn't deny the mounting unease within him.

In a bid to alleviate his discomfort, Ben's friend offered him a cup of water. Ben's hands shook as he brought the cup to his lips, gulping down the water in desperation. But the combination of heightened emotions and swirling thoughts proved overwhelming. Suddenly, everything went black, and Ben fainted.

When Ben stepped out of his home that morning, he felt perfectly fine. Yet, as he encountered a series of friends each emphasizing his deteriorating condition, his own mind played a cruel trick on him. Fueled by his friends' insinuations, his imagination led him to experience the very symptoms they described.

Ben's story underscores how easily our minds can succumb to imaginative narratives, especially when fueled by external suggestions. It also highlights the role of collective influence—the more people emphasize a certain narrative, the more real it can become to the individual. This phenomenon serves as a reminder that understanding that the interplay between our thoughts, fears, and external influences is essential to navigating the complexities of our minds. By recognizing these dynamics, we can work toward gaining better control over our thoughts and emotions, ultimately leading to a more informed and balanced perspective on our fears and anxieties.

Investigate Your Fears

I once had a friend who harbored an intense fear of entering elevators, driven by the apprehension of becoming trapped. However, life has a curious way of confronting us with our deepest fears, and one day he found himself in a situation that challenged his anxiety head-on. Despite his dread of confinement, he was compelled to step into an elevator due to a pressing business engagement. On that day, his concern about being stuck with his financial bills overshadowed his fear of getting stuck in the elevator.

As fate would have it, his misgivings materialized when the elevator came to an abrupt halt between floors. Panic surged through the passengers as they struggled to comprehend their predicament. Urgent calls for help reverberated within the confined space as they implored passersby to summon emergency services. Amid the frenzy, an unexpected transformation took place within my friend. Instead of succumbing to distress, he emerged as the most resolute individual in the group, unswayed by fear.

With unwavering determination, my friend shifted his focus from anxiety to finding a solution. He surveyed the interior of the elevator, his gaze landing on a button conveniently located at the bottom panel—a button designed precisely for situations like these. The button, when pressed, would alert emergency services, promptly summoning the fire department to their aid. Acting swiftly, my friend pressed the button without hesitation, initiating a sequence of events that led to their swift rescue.

Reflecting on his experience, my friend approached me with a sense of enlightenment. He pondered how he managed to remain composed in a scenario that once consumed him with dread. It was then that I shared a perspective on fear—a perspective rooted in understanding and knowledge. I explained to him that often fear stems from a lack of information, allowing our imagination to fill the void. It's human nature to imagine the worst when faced with the unknown. For instance, my friend's fear of being stuck in an elevator amplified his dread, yet he never considered investigating what actually happens when elevators malfunction. His vivid imagination conjured scenarios of helplessness and panic, but when confronted with the reality of the situation, he exhibited remarkable composure.

The story of my friend's elevator experience underscored a powerful principle: that many fears are rooted in misinformation and lack of awareness. When we encounter a fear head-on and gather knowledge about it, the fear often loses its grip on us. In essence, knowledge serves as a potent antidote to fear, disarming its potency and allowing us to navigate challenges with a sense of confidence.

Consider the connection between OCD and fear. OCD cannot thrive unless it's linked to a fear. For instance, consider a person who repeatedly checks the door every few minutes. This behavior can't persist if they are absolutely certain that no intruder will enter the house. There must be a connection to a concern as the status of the door being open or closed wouldn't matter if there were no possibility of an intruder entering the house.

This fact holds significant importance because eliminating the fear can unravel the entire foundation of the obsession. I'm presenting this not as a universal solution, recognizing that some individuals require more in-depth techniques that I won't delve into for the sake of simplicity. However, by encouraging individuals to identify the fear or concern driving their obsession, they might discover that these fears and concerns are often unfounded. I bring this up because I've come across numerous instances where people obsessively repeated certain actions to ensure correctness, only to realize later that these actions weren't necessary to begin with. It's their imagination that constructs a belief dictating the necessity of certain actions to ensure or prevent something, even though these beliefs are founded on non-existent realities.

For example, imagine someone who constantly feels compelled to double-check if they've locked the front door. This person might believe that their house will be vulnerable to break-ins if they don't ensure the door is locked perfectly. However, upon closer examination, they realize that their neighborhood has an extremely low crime rate and their house is equipped with a sophisticated security system. The fear of a break-in is largely unfounded, yet their imagination has created a belief that excessive door-checking is necessary for their security. In this case, the fear driving the obsession doesn't align with the reality of their situation.

Or imagine someone who constantly checks if their stove is turned off before leaving their home. They believe that if they don't double or triple-check, their house might catch fire. However, upon closer examination, they realize that their stove is equipped with an automatic shut-off feature and even if it were left on, the chances of a fire starting are extremely slim. The fear of a potential fire is a product of their imagination, and the concern driving their obsession is not based in reality.

It's crucial to recognize that we're not alone in our fears or problems. Countless individuals have faced similar challenges and emerged with valuable insights. This realization leads us to an essential rule of thumb: when confronted with a problem or fear, we're not the first to experience it. Others have traversed this path before us, and their solutions are readily available.

In today's interconnected world, gathering information has become increasingly accessible. A simple Google search can provide a wealth of knowledge about almost any subject. This modern convenience empowers us to overcome fears and obstacles through education. By tapping into the collective wisdom of humanity, we can liberate ourselves from the clutches of fear and anxiety.

In conclusion, my friend's elevator ordeal shed light on the transformative power of knowledge in dismantling fear. By confronting his dread and understanding the mechanics of the situation, he triumphed over his anxiety. This story serves as a reminder that seeking knowledge is a potent tool for alleviating fears and overcoming challenges. When we arm ourselves with understanding, we discover that solutions exist, waiting to be uncovered by those who dare to confront their fears with curiosity and determination.

Practice Compassion in the Face of Others' Fears

While we're discussing fears, I'd like to address family members who have a loved one grappling with severe and irrational fears. Although this book primarily focuses on everyday problems that many people experience, it's crucial to touch upon an important aspect. Specifically, it's advised not to dismiss or mock the fears of individuals, even if those fears seem implausible or exaggerated. By doing so, you inadvertently create a sense of isolation for them, leaving them feeling unappreciated and misunderstood.

For example, consider a scenario where someone imagines an impending heart attack. If, as a family member, you respond with laughter, it can lead to unintended consequences. This person may fear that you won't take their fears seriously enough to seek medical help promptly, which can exacerbate their anxiety and distress. The act of laughing at their concerns can amplify their perception of vulnerability, making them question whether they can truly rely on you during times of crisis.

In such cases, showing empathy and providing reassurance are essential. Recognize that the experience of fear is subjective and complex and that what might seem irrational to others can be very real and overwhelming for the person experiencing it. By offering a supportive and understanding response, you contribute to their overall well-being and help alleviate the heightened anxiety that their fears can bring. This approach fosters an environment where they feel safe discussing their fears openly, reducing the risk of unnecessary stress and isolation.

I recall a situation when I offered some advice to an individual who was absolutely convinced that he was suffering from a serious illness. Remarkably, despite undergoing multiple medical tests that consistently indicated his good health, this person's unwavering belief in a hidden ailment persisted. In attempting to convey my perspective, I mentioned that he might be in a more intricate predicament compared to an individual who genuinely faced the illness he fears.

The rationale behind this assertion lies in the observation that someone who is genuinely afflicted with a specific ailment often discovers an extraordinary wellspring of inner resilience that aids them through the trying times. This strength becomes an essential coping mechanism. Additionally, these individuals are blessed with the unwavering support of their loved ones who rally around them, providing comfort and encouragement during their journey toward recovery.

In contrast, when one grapples with unwarranted fears and anxieties, the landscape shifts considerably. The absence of a definitive medical diagnosis does not diminish the emotional intensity of these fears. Yet, what truly magnifies the complexity of this experience is the sense of solitude it brings. Struggling with fears in isolation, without the presence of understanding and empathetic companions, can be deeply distressing.

Sharing these worries with family members is fraught with its own set of challenges. There's the underlying concern that loved ones might not fully grasp the depth of these anxieties or might dismiss them altogether. Consequently, one might choose to shoulder these burdens independently, navigating through their apprehensions without external guidance or support.

It's important to recognize that mental and emotional battles are as valid as physical ailments, often exerting a comparable toll on an individual's well-being. Acknowledging the significance of seeking solace and counsel from those who care can initiate a transformative journey toward healing. While the struggle may not be immediately visible, its impact can be monumental. This underscores the necessity of cultivating an environment where mental health concerns are met with compassion and understanding, ultimately reinforcing the strength of collective understanding and empathy.

When facing the daily battles that arise when fear enters the picture, take a moment to reflect on the ways you've dealt with fear in the past. Though your fears may show up differently in various contexts, you have bravely faced the emotion before and found solutions for how to cope with or eliminate fear entirely. Equip yourself with the knowledge and perspective necessary to face the fears that arise most commonly in your life. Write them down and talk them out with a trusted friend. Just like how you overcame the fear of the dark as a kid, you can use your experience and knowledge to overcome whatever fear you face today.

CHAPTER 8

EXERCISE
SELF-CONTROL

Temper Anger through Measured Expectations

Exercising self-control when anger threatens to overpower us is a vital skill that enables us to take on challenging situations with grace and composure. Reflecting on past instances where I successfully tempered my anger reveals common threads of mindfulness, empathy, and an intentional effort to understand the broader context. In those moments, I recognized that reacting impulsively would only exacerbate the situation. By tempering my expectations and acknowledging that not everything will unfold according to my wishes, I gained a valuable perspective that allowed me to approach conflicts with a level head.

Understanding that we have the power to choose our responses to anger empowers us to redirect that energy constructively. This practice not only builds healthier relationships but also reinforces the idea that self-control is a powerful tool in navigating life's challenges, offering a pathway to personal growth and more harmonious interactions.

Assess Your Expectations of Others

A man approached me seeking guidance for his overwhelming anger issues that were negatively affecting his relationship. He expressed genuine concern that if he didn't address this problem, it could ultimately lead to the demise of his marriage. In an effort to understand the nature of his anger, I inquired about his most recent outburst.

He recounted an incident from the previous day when he returned home to find the dishes unwashed and the house in disarray. The frustration he felt was overpowering, and he confessed to reacting with an intensity that he himself found alarming. I probed further, asking if there had been a time in the past when he encountered a similarly messy house but managed to maintain his composure.

After a moment of reflection, he recalled an instance when he had returned home to an even messier house but hadn't experienced the same level of anger. When asked what he believed had triggered the difference in his reactions, he struggled to pinpoint the exact reason. However, he did mention that during that particular episode, he had anticipated the disorder and messiness.

That's when the breakthrough came. I pointed out that the only significant difference between those two instances was his level of expectation. In the first scenario, he had expected the house to be in order and was caught off guard by the chaos. In the second scenario, he had mentally prepared himself for the messiness and had consequently managed to maintain his calm.

It was a revelation for him. He realized that his own mind had offered him a solution in the past, a technique of preemptive self-calming through lowered expectations, but he had inadvertently forgotten about it. The essence of his solution was simple: manage expectations. He had subconsciously employed this technique before, and it had worked. The challenge now was to make it a conscious practice.

I shared with him a practical approach to implementing this technique into his daily routine. I suggested that he take a pen and paper and write down the following affirmation: "I do not expect the house to be clean when I come home. Further, I am prepared to respond to any situation that might enrage me by pausing and reevaluating my expectations." This written reminder would serve as a mental anchor, helping him remember his own insight when he faced triggering situations.

The key to overcoming moments of intense anger is to remain open to introspection, willing to learn from our past experiences, and committed to implementing these insights into our daily lives. In doing so, we can transform moments of frustration into opportunities for growth and positive change. If you notice yourself frequently getting angry about something, make an effort to recall times when that situation didn't trigger your anger. Reflect on the thought that helped you diffuse that anger and put it into writing. By doing this, you'll equip yourself to maintain your composure whenever those situations arise.

This approach, although seemingly straightforward, has greater implications. It's a testament to the power of our own minds to offer us solutions when we need them the most. By recognizing the strategy he had unconsciously used in the past, the man was empowered to take control of his reactions and prevent his anger from escalating. In this case, the technique of managing expectations proved to be a powerful tool in preventing anger from spiraling out of control. As we embark on our own journeys of self-improvement, let us remain open to the wisdom that lies within us and use it to create more peaceful and fulfilling lives.

Recognize When Your Anger Is Directed Inward

Once, when meeting with a school principal, he confided in me about a teacher who had become an enigma within the school walls. This educator bore an unexpected flaw in his teaching approach. When his students didn't immediately understand the material in the way he taught it, an inexplicable transformation overcame him, causing his patience to dissolve into frustration and his voice to escalate. In exasperation, he would exclaim, "Why don't you understand?"

Listening intently, I understood that this teacher was grappling with a conundrum that transcended mere teaching techniques. I had a hunch that the layers of his frustration were entwined with the fabric of his own understanding of the subject matter he sought to impart. Recognizing the complexity of the situation, I assured the principal that I was ready to help.

The principal broached the subject with the teacher, urging him to seek counsel. Reluctance and hesitation echoed in the teacher's response, but the principal's insistence was an unwavering plea. The teacher approached me with a mix of curiosity and skepticism in his eyes. His opening words betrayed his guarded stance: "I'm not sure what magic you have up your sleeve, but the principal seems convinced that you can help me."

With a smile, I responded, "No magic, just a desire to understand and assist."

As the conversation unfolded, I got a glimpse into the teacher's psyche. His self-assessment was a medley of contradictions; his boasts of success were punctuated with pockets of frustration. "I consider myself a successful teacher in many aspects," he began, "but I must confess that I lose my patience when my students struggle to grasp my explanations."

The observations he shared were insightful, yet they were shadows cast by a deeper, less-explored realm. With gentle probing, I ventured into an unconventional line of inquiry, "Do you fully understand the teachings yourself?"

The question seemed to touch a chord within him, and his response carried a note of introspection. "It's interesting that you ask that," he began, "because I often find myself grappling with my own understanding of the subject matter."

The revelation was the key that unlocked the door to his vexation. As our conversation delved into the depths of his frustration, it became evident that his impatience was intertwined with his internal struggle. He bore the weight of his own perceived limitations, his irritations mirroring the discontent he felt within himself.

The pieces of the puzzle began to fall into place. His anger at his students' lack of comprehension was, in essence, an echo of his inner turmoil. In my arsenal of advice, I recalled the statement of a wise friend, Pinchus Friedman, who had imparted a pearl of insight, "Remember, sometimes when you're angry at someone, you're really angry at yourself."

Guided by this principle, I invited the teacher to embark on a journey of self-discovery. We unraveled the threads of his own learning process, exploring the root of his perceived gaps in comprehension. In this exploration, he found not just answers but the path to a solution.

Piece by piece, we reconstructed his understanding, weaving clarity and coherence into the fabric of his knowledge. Together, we unveiled strategies to address his personal roadblocks, transforming his uncertainties into stepping stones toward a renewed sense of mastery.

As our time together drew to a close, the teacher exhaled a sigh of relief. A palpable weight had been lifted, replaced by a renewed sense of confidence and purpose. The transformation that had begun was undeniable, a testament to the power of unraveling one's own complexities to effect change in the world around us.

In the days that followed, the school witnessed a remarkable transformation. The teacher who had once expressed his frustrations through raised voices and impatient gestures was now a beacon of calm. He found solace in the understanding that his students' struggles were not merely theirs to bear but reflections of his own journey. With this newfound insight, he became a guiding light and a patient and compassionate presence in his classroom.

In navigating and mastering the emotion of anger, it's essential to acknowledge that frustration and anger are natural human responses. Yet, delving deeper, you might find that getting angry at yourself for feeling anger can intensify the emotion. Remember, being angry about why you're angry is much harder to overcome than the original anger. Embrace your humanity and the spectrum of emotions that come with it. By doing so, you're not only expressing empathy to others but also extending compassion to yourself.

In a world where emotions can be unpredictable and reactions can sometimes feel overpowering, looking inward at the root of your anger equips you with a valuable toolkit. Through understanding yourself, you build self-compassion and emotional resilience. As you journey through the labyrinth of human interactions, remember that these insights act as guiding lights, steering you away from impulsive reactions and toward a more amicable connection with both others and yourself.

Realize the Strength of Restraint

The principal beamed at the transformation: the teacher once ensnared by his own internal discord now emerged as a shining example of patience. As the principal and I talked through the results, the principal's eyes shone with a glint of curiosity. He wished to glean insights on yet another challenge that had begun to weave its narrative within the school's walls—the issue of some boys engaged in frequent skirmishes. The constant clashes had cast a disruptive shadow over the learning environment. The boys who carried an unwavering commitment to winning at any cost continually fueled the turbulence.

My mind drifted back to a similar issue I was asked to mediate: a child who seemed to perceive every utterance as a challenge to his pride. His retorts were swift and sharp, even in the face of minor provocations. A pattern emerged of a young spirit yearning to assert his strength and uphold his perceived status as a winner. Drawing on this memory, I wove a narrative that mirrored the principal's quandary. A tale where parents approached me, their voices trembling with concern over a child who seemed to channel every disagreement into a full-blown confrontation. It was clear that beneath the veneer of these skirmishes lay a deeper longing: a desire to stand tall as a victor.

With this dynamic setting the stage, I shared with the principal the guidance I had had provided to those parents long ago. It revolved around a delicate dance of conversations—a parent chosen for their close connection with the child engaged in a heart-to-heart dialogue with me during a calm interlude. It was in this tranquil moment that transformation found its footing. Within the discourse, the parent drew from their own history, revealing a shift in perception that time had nurtured. "In my youth," they recounted, "I believed that fighting back was the ultimate display of strength. I thought that by meeting fire with fire, I was showing resilience and mettle. But as the years went by, I came to realize that true strength comes from the mastery of one's impulses. The true victory lies not in reacting but in exercising restraint. I learned that every time I chose not to respond to provocation, I felt a deeper sense of strength and control."

The principal absorbed this notion with palpable interest, the concept a stark departure from conventional norms of punishment. This was a pivot from external conquest to internal sovereignty, a reframing of the constructs of triumph and defeat, of power and vulnerability. The principal, intrigued and eager, vowed to infuse this approach into the school's fabric. True to his commitment, he touched base again, his voice tinged with an undeniable eagerness. The technique had taken root, and not just in the one-on-one interaction with the specific student. The principal had seized the opportunity to address the entire student body, sharing the newfound wisdom that had blossomed from our conversation.

In the ensuing days, a cultural shift seemed to ripple through the school's corridors. The boys, prompted by the new perspective, engaged in self-reflection. A new definition of "winner" and "loser" began to take shape, one that valued restraint over reaction. In the end, it was a triumph of empathy over impulse, a testament to the transformation that awaited those willing to redefine their narratives. It was a reminder that transformation, like the delicate unfurling of a flower, is a journey that carries its own sense of gratification.

As our conversation ebbed, I was left with a heartwarming affirmation that even amidst the complexities of human behavior, a simple shift in perspective could spark a domino effect of change. And as I bid the principal farewell, I was reminded that sometimes, the stories we share hold within them the power to shape lives, one perspective at a time.

Don't Cross the Red Lines

Arguing in a relationship is never a healthy sign, but what's even more detrimental is when those arguments spiral out of control. It's crucial to remember that there are red lines you should never cross, as crossing them can have dire consequences for your relationship. Recognizing and respecting these boundaries is essential to maintaining a healthy connection with your partner.

While disagreements are a natural part of any relationship, it's important to acknowledge that certain limits should never be breached. You may have experienced moments when anger gets the best of you, tempting you to say hurtful things. However, just as you wouldn't willingly jump into a fire, don't let your anger drive you to cross those red lines. Why risk playing with emotional fire?

Understanding your personal red lines is crucial, but equally important is recognizing the potential danger of crossing them. Sometimes, in the heat of the moment, we may underestimate the power of our words. The analogy holds: don't let your belief that you can easily take back hurtful words mislead you. Even wiser individuals have fallen victim to this trap, believing they can weather the storm they create. The truth is, once you cross that red line, the damage can be irreversible.

I don't mean to alarm you, but it's vital to emphasize the gravity of this situation. The words that cross the red line aren't just part of an argument—they can lead to the unraveling of your relationship. It might not happen instantly, but it marks the beginning of a gradual decline. These hurtful words seep into the subconscious, creating a foundation of doubt and negativity that erodes the bond between partners.

As an optimist, I believe in the potential for growth and healing within relationships. However, I must stress that crossing the red line is a perilous path that can lead to an irreversible breakdown. Maintaining open communication, respecting boundaries, and avoiding hurtful words are key to preserving the health and longevity of your relationship. Every word we choose matters and has the power to shape the course of our connection with our loved ones.

When discussing the importance of healthy relationships, it's essential to highlight the value of self-control. Beyond just being a commendable virtue, self-control forms the very foundation of strong relationships. While it might be tempting to respond in the heat of the moment, the repercussions can have a lasting impression. Moreover, practicing self-control has a remarkable effect on boosting your self-esteem. The ability to restrain yourself not only brings instant rewards but also provides a sense of accomplishment that far outweighs the fleeting satisfaction of having the final say. In essence, exercising self-control contributes significantly to building meaningful and harmonious connections.

Take a Beat to Think about the Other Side

The ability to understand someone's perspective grants you a broader view of their actions, their motivations, and the context surrounding their behavior. This broader perspective acts as a buffer, preventing immediate emotional reactions and allowing for a more measured response. However, an equally vital aspect is understanding yourself.

I'd like to highlight a crucial aspect of this emotion. Taking a moment to truly understand others and stepping into their perspective holds incredible value. Not only does it benefit the individuals we might be quick to judge, but it also brings advantages to us.

By making the effort to empathize and see things from someone else's point of view, we create an environment of compassion and open-mindedness. This practice has the remarkable power to prevent a plethora of conflicts and difficulties that stem from misunderstandings and unfounded judgments.

Think about it: how often have we experienced frustration or anger because we didn't fully understand where someone was coming from? Taking that extra step to understand their motivations, struggles, and feelings can diffuse tension and replace it with empathy.

In essence, practicing empathy acts as a two-way gift. Not only do we offer understanding to others, but we also free ourselves from the clutches of anger and resentment. So, the next time you feel anger welling up, consider taking a moment to understand the other person's perspective. It might just be the key to a more peaceful interaction.

Anger is a powerful emotion that, if left unchecked, can wreak havoc in our lives and relationships. When we don't focus on practicing self-control, we let the feeling of the moment overtake our whole being. This foolishly keeps us from taking a moment to look back on our past experiences to try to diffuse our anger and approach situations with a level head and calm disposition. While acting on anger seems to feel right and be appropriate in certain situations, it rarely offers the long-term solution that will lead to our greatest well-being. By digging deeper into our motivation, expectations, and past experiences, we will discover unique strategies that dismantle anger and provide alternate responses that allow us to address the situation with a calm and collected disposition.

CHAPTER 9

SEEK CLARITY
IN THE FOG

Dispel Gloom through Introspection

The path to clarity isn't merely a search for solutions; it's a personal adventure, a purposeful unraveling of the uncertainties that darken our comprehension. Venturing into self-reflection, we unveil the secrets that cloud our perspective, carving a route to enlightenment and lifting the shadows obscuring the truths within. This journey prompts us to face the vague facets of our being, leading to an exploration of self-discovery and a quest for clarity.

In moments of gloom and sadness, it may seem as if these emotions have a permanent hold on us, appearing out of nowhere. However, reflecting on past experiences reminds us that these states are transient. Gloom is not an enduring destination but rather a passing cloud. Delving deeper into the thoughts that lead us into these moments of darkness can accelerate the journey toward clarity. By understanding the triggers and patterns, we gain the ability to navigate through gloom more swiftly, transforming it from an overwhelming force into a fleeting visitor on our path to a clearer mental landscape.

Look below the Surface

One teacher's satisfaction with my previous advice prompted him to
open up about another predicament that was causing disturbances in
both his life and the classroom. He confided that he often woke up
with a cloud of negativity hanging over him, which inevitably affected
his interactions with his students. This issue was like a shadow he
couldn't shake, dimming his enthusiasm for teaching and casting a
pall over the day ahead.

Curious to delve deeper into this emotional puzzle, I inquired
about his emotional landscape during these early hours. He described
feeling a mixture of frustration and helplessness, unsure of why he
couldn't shake off these morning blues. It was as if an invisible weight
anchored him down, influencing his interactions with both his
students and colleagues. The heaviness was palpable, and it was taking
a toll on the vibrant energy he wished to exude.

Recognizing that emotions often have an underlying thought
component, I gently guided him to consider that perhaps there was a
thought pattern he was overlooking. I suggested that emotions, even
negative ones, can be indicators of subconscious thoughts that might
not immediately surface. These thoughts, lurking in the depths of the
mind, can have a lasting impact on our mood without our conscious
awareness.

In an attempt to untangle this emotional knot, I offered a simple
yet transformative exercise. The next time he found himself awaken-
ing to a sour mood, I suggested he take a step back and reflect on the
experiences and interactions he had encountered over the past twenty-
four hours. By examining these events, he might uncover the elusive
negative thought that was acting as the catalyst for his morning gloom.

His initial skepticism dissolved as he grasped the potential of this exercise. He agreed to give it a try, intrigued by the idea that by confronting his thoughts, he could regain control over his emotions. This was an invitation to look beyond the surface, to delve into the layers of his mind and unearth the thoughts that had been stealthily shaping his mood. To guide him in the process, I provided an additional technique. I recommended that he create a journal specifically dedicated to this practice. Each morning, upon waking, he could jot down his prevailing thoughts and emotions. This would serve as a written record, enabling him to track patterns over time. It would provide a visual insight into the ebb and flow of his emotions and eventually reveal the elusive thought patterns that lay beneath.

As we explored this technique, I shared anecdotes of others who had benefited from similar practices. Many were astounded by the stark contrast between the thoughts they held and the rationality they valued once they saw their musings written out. Some even exclaimed, "Did I truly think this way?" This process of writing down their thoughts provided a reality check, a means of externalizing their internal dialogue and subjecting it to critical examination.

In the weeks that followed, the teacher engaged wholeheartedly in this practice. He embraced the habit of recording his thoughts and emotions each morning, forming a daily ritual of self-awareness. Gradually, he began to recognize recurring themes, threads of thought that wove through his days and colored his interactions. Through this journaling process, he began to gain insight into the origins of his morning negativity.

One entry revealed a pattern of dwelling on past mistakes, even those that were minor. This tendency to replay errors and missteps in his mind was a major contributor to his recurring negative moods. Armed with awareness, he found it easier to shift his focus from the past to the present moment, effectively curbing this counterproductive habit.

In the midst of his self-discovery journey, the teacher began to experience a notable shift. He found himself waking up with a renewed sense of clarity and purpose. As he dissected his thoughts on paper, he was able to pinpoint the sources of his negative emotions. Armed with this insight, he started to rewrite his mental script, consciously choosing positive affirmations and intentions for the day ahead.

During our subsequent meetings, he shared the effect this practice had on his well-being. The clouds of negativity that once shrouded his mornings began to dissipate, replaced by a sense of clarity and positivity. He was able to enter his classroom with renewed enthusiasm, and his interactions with his students became more authentic and uplifting. This transformation extended beyond his professional life. He noticed that as he gained control over his thoughts, his overall outlook on life brightened. The technique of writing down his thoughts and analyzing them objectively had enabled him to unravel deeply ingrained patterns and replace them with empowering beliefs.

In our final conversation, the teacher expressed gratitude for the technique that had altered the course of his mornings and, subsequently, his days. He marveled at how something as seemingly mundane as journaling had the power to reshape his mindset and elevate his emotional well-being.

As we bid farewell, I left him with a reminder that the tools for growth and transformation often lie within us, waiting to be unearthed. In his journey from morning gloom to morning glow, he had harnessed the power of introspection and self-awareness, serving as a testament to the remarkable potential that resides within each of us.

Amid life's chance encounters, I found myself strolling down a bustling street corner when I chanced upon the school principal once more. His face, typically a picture of professionalism, was now adorned with a genuine smile that spoke volumes. "You know," he began with an air of contentment, "that teacher you offered your wisdom to? He's turned over a new leaf, or perhaps a whole new chapter."

Mindful introspection and intentional awareness of our thoughts and emotions can help us navigate through recurring negative thought processes and emotional patterns that result in us becoming stuck. While it may initially be difficult to enforce the daily practice of journaling your thoughts and feelings, it will eventually become part of your routine, and you will be thankful for the ability to look back and see patterns and connections that would've been a challenge to piece together otherwise.

Prove Yourself Wrong

In every story, in every encounter, lay the potential for transformation—a journey that begins with introspection and unfolds through understanding. I once encountered an individual burdened by an incessant belief that all her efforts were destined for failure. Her mind was fixated on the worst-case scenarios, fearing the worst outcome in every situation. At first, I grappled with how to transform such a deeply ingrained mindset, one that anticipated doom with every step.

However, a similar situation from the past offered guidance. I recalled a conversation with someone who harbored similar apprehensions. I had advised him to chronicle instances where he had feared doom, only to find that things turned out positively. This exercise involved writing down all the times he anticipated failure, only to be proven wrong when situations unfolded favorably. The result? A considerable list of instances where his pessimistic predictions fell flat.

Upon reflection, I realized that this method could be applied to the current individual struggling with pessimism. I urged her to undertake the same exercise—to compile a record of instances when she predicted doom, but events unfolded contrary to her expectations. Much like the previous case, the exercise yielded an extensive list that showcased how frequently her fears had been unfounded.

Witnessing the undeniable evidence of her own track record—the times she had assumed doom but experienced success—inspired a shift in perspective. The realization that her concerns were often misplaced sowed the seeds of change. Just as the previous person had been astonished by the stark contrast between his perceived outcomes and actual outcomes, this individual, too, underwent a significant transformation in her thinking.

This parallel experience demonstrated the efficacy of a practical approach in reshaping cognitive patterns. The act of cataloging instances of misjudgment offered tangible proof that the "doomed" mindset didn't always reflect reality. In both cases, the individuals' attitudes underwent dramatic change. They began to recognize that while the habit of anticipating doom was deeply ingrained, it was far from accurate.

These situations underscore the potential of self-awareness and reflection in altering our thought processes. The exercise of challenging negative assumptions with evidence from one's own life can dismantle even the most entrenched beliefs. By revealing the contrast between perception and reality, this method empowers individuals to break free from the cycle of pessimism and embrace a more balanced and hopeful outlook.

I encourage you to keep an ongoing list of events in your life that resulted in favor and success. Not only will this result in evidence to help you look on the positive side of things and dispel gloom or feelings of pending doom, but it will also help you develop an attitude of gratitude that will positively change your life and outlook.

Find the Silver Lining

Often, even when things don't go our way and sadness overtakes us for a season, there are pockets of hope and lessons in the challenge that bring greater clarity and understanding. In the midst of challenging seasons or disappointments, actively seeking the silver lining becomes your path out. It's during these dark periods that the pursuit of positivity and lessons in adversity can lead to extensive personal growth. Embracing the idea that every cloud has a silver lining encourages a mindset shift, propelling us forward through difficult times. Instead of succumbing to despair, we become architects of our own resilience, extracting valuable insights that shape not only our immediate experiences but also contribute to the ongoing development of our character and perspective. This proactive approach not only accelerates our journey through the shadows but also ensures that, on the other side, we emerge stronger, wiser, and more attuned to the brighter aspects of life.

In the heart of a bustling city, there lived a woman named Sophia who had an extraordinary ability to find silver linings in the darkest of clouds. One day, she unexpectedly lost her job, sending her world into a tailspin. As she navigated the daunting prospect of unemployment, Sophia decided to channel her energy into volunteering at a local community center.

There she encountered a diverse group of individuals facing their own challenges—some grappling with homelessness, others with unemployment like herself. Instead of succumbing to despair, Sophia began organizing workshops and skill-building sessions at the center, leveraging her professional expertise.

As she poured her passion into helping others, something remarkable happened. Sophia discovered a sense of fulfillment and purpose she had never experienced in her previous job. The community center became a hub of empowerment, where people learned new skills, found support, and built a sense of camaraderie.

Word spread about Sophia's transformative work, catching the attention of a philanthropic organization dedicated to community development. They offered her the opportunity to lead a city-wide initiative aimed at creating sustainable programs for those facing adversity.

Sophia's journey, from the depths of job loss to becoming a catalyst for positive change, not only turned her life around but became an inspiring example of finding silver linings in the face of adversity. Her story, featured in a best-selling self-help book, serves as a beacon of hope, encouraging readers to seek opportunities for growth and positivity even in the most challenging situations.

Through better understanding how we responded to gloomy seasons and moods in the past, we can more quickly work our way out of the fog of gloom and down the path of clarity and self-awareness. Understanding our historical reactions provides valuable insights into our emotional landscape, allowing us to identify patterns and triggers. Armed with this self-awareness, we can develop targeted strategies to overcome despair, turning gloom into an opportunity for growth and self-discovery. The retrospective exploration not only expedites our journey toward clarity but also equips us with a greater capacity for resilience, ensuring that when future gloomy seasons arise, we possess the tools and insights to traverse the darkness with a greater sense of purpose and understanding.

CHAPTER 10
EXTEND SELF-COMPASSION

Replace Unreasonable Guilt with Realistic Standards

Guilt is a powerful emotion that can easily crush us with its weight. When we go through life feeling guilty for all we're not doing or for the things we've done in the past, it considerably reduces our ability to live a fulfilling and joyful life. To overcome these feelings of intense guilt and ensure that they are not controlling us, we need to not just try to avoid them or not think about them but rather to face them head on and overcome them through logic and self-compassion.

We have all faced overwhelming guilt in the past and have overcome it, so all we have to do is look back on what in the past helped us overcome the guilt and apply that to our current feelings.

Forgive Yourself for Past Mistakes

We have all done things we regret doing and felt guilty about. Guilt is a helpful tool in guiding us toward changing our behavior and helping us improve ourselves. However, when guilt becomes an all-encompassing force, it can result in isolation, low self-esteem, and

chaotic behavior. Guilt is supposed to help us take the action necessary to right our wrongs as much as we are able and learn from the
experience; it is supposed to be transient, not enduring. In the face of
our regrets and past mistakes, we need to be able to forgive ourselves
in order to move forward and remove the guilt that weighs on us.

Abraham Lincoln, the sixteenth President of the United States,
faced numerous setbacks and personal failures throughout his life.
One notable example is his political career before becoming president. Lincoln experienced defeats in elections, bankruptcy, and the
loss of his young son.

One of the most renowned moments in Lincoln's life is his ability
to persevere and learn from his mistakes. Despite facing significant
personal and professional challenges, he continued to strive for success.
Lincoln's capacity to forgive himself for past political and personal
setbacks played a crucial role in his resilience and ultimate ascent to
the presidency. His journey from adversity to leadership serves as a
powerful historical example of how forgiving oneself for past mistakes
and embracing personal growth can lead to remarkable achievements.

Rather than letting guilt fester, filling his head with shame and
self-loathing, Lincoln decided to own his mistakes and put them
behind him so they wouldn't become roadblocks to his future. If there
is a mistake that you've made that has become a personal roadblock
to your potential, I encourage you to recognize it and own it today.
Through directly addressing it, you can extend self-forgiveness and
self-compassion in order to move past it.

Challenge the Feeling of Not Doing Enough

In a world brimming with responsibilities and connections, it's not uncommon to find ourselves ensnared by the web of unreasonable guilt. Such was the case when I encountered an individual who carried a heavy burden of guilt, seemingly without reason. This person was tormented by guilt—guilt that he wasn't doing enough for his children, siblings, and parents. He carried the weight of guilt for not caring enough, even though he desperately cared.

In an effort to untangle this complex emotion, I proposed a simple exercise. I suggested that he jot down what he did for the people he felt guilty about and also list what he believed he should be doing more. This act of putting thoughts to paper transformed his perception. As he reviewed his comprehensive list, he was struck by the realization of the substantial efforts he was already investing in his relationships. He also acknowledged that certain circumstances lay beyond his control, leading him to question the validity of his unreasonable guilt.

Prompting further reflection, I posed a question: "If a close friend presented you with this very list, detailing their actions and aspirations, would you admonish them for their perceived shortcomings?" The response was an unequivocal no. The individual recognized that understanding and compassion would guide his response to a friend's similar situation, highlighting the inherent humanity in striving to balance numerous commitments.

Addressing another facet of his guilt, I painted a scenario: could he conceive of a person who didn't care yet felt guilty about not caring? The smile that formed illuminated a vital truth: the very act of pondering one's emotions indicated an underlying care that he had doubted.

Returning to a pivotal strategy, I asked if he had moments when guilt didn't overshadow his thoughts. The individual confirmed that, indeed, he had experienced such clarity. It was during these times that he had reflected on the very list before him. I pointed out the curious phenomenon—how often individuals approach me with problems they've already resolved, only to let the solution slip from memory, leaving them mired in negativity. It was at this juncture that I urged him to take this list and transcribe it until its contents became etched in his memory, like an anchor to ground him during moments of unreasonable guilt.

Clarity often eludes us in the midst of complex feelings. Through self-reflection and compassionate perspective, we have the power to untangle these emotional knots, crafting a narrative that resonates with understanding, self-acceptance, and the recognition of our shared human experience.

Recognize the Bounds of Human Limitation

In a similar story, a woman played the roles of a devoted mother, a caring sister, and a loving daughter. Despite her heartfelt commitment to her family, she carried an overwhelming burden of guilt. This guilt manifested in her belief that she wasn't dedicating enough time to her children, wasn't supporting her siblings adequately, and wasn't meeting the standards of care she felt her aging parents deserved.

One day, she found herself alone in her garden, her heart heavy with an almost insurmountable weight of unreasonable guilt. The guilt seemed to press upon her, making it difficult to breathe. She reflected on the moments she had missed with her children due to her demanding job, the times she couldn't be there for her siblings, and the instances when she believed she fell short as a daughter.

Overwhelmed by her emotions, she decided to confide in a close friend. She poured out her feelings, describing her struggles and the persistent guilt that consumed her. As she spoke, her friend listened with empathy, understanding the depth of her pain.

Following a thoughtful pause, her friend gently encouraged her to create a list of all the ways she had contributed to her family, both big and small. Initially hesitant, she picked up a pen and started documenting every act of kindness, each sacrifice, and every effort she had devoted to her relationships.

As she gazed at the list, something within her shifted. The evidence of her love and care was right there on paper. She realized that she had shouldered an irrational burden, holding herself to standards that were unattainable. With tears in her eyes, she whispered, "I didn't realize the extent of my efforts until I saw them written down."

Her friend smiled and posed a question that would forever change her perspective: "If you were to read this list authored by someone else, what advice would you offer them?" Taking a moment to reflect, she responded, "I would tell them that they're doing their best, that they're human, and they can't possibly do everything."

Her friend nodded with understanding in her eyes. "Precisely," she said softly. "You're no exception. You're a devoted mother, a supportive sister, and a loving daughter. You're putting in your best effort, just like anyone else."

In that poignant moment, the weight she had been carrying began to lift. She realized that her guilt had stemmed from unreasonable expectations she had placed upon herself. She understood that she couldn't be present everywhere at once, and this realization didn't diminish her care or dedication.

From that day on, she kept the list as a reminder. Whenever she felt the tendrils of unreasonable guilt creeping in, she would revisit the list, using it as a touchstone to remind herself of her efforts. She recognized that guilt wasn't a measure of her love; rather, it was a signal of her humanity.

This story serves as a powerful reminder of how we tend to judge ourselves far more harshly than we would judge others. Her journey from overwhelming guilt to self-compassion and understanding exemplifies the transformative power of perspective. Additionally, it underscores the influence that a supportive friend can have on our lives.

When you find yourself ensnared by the suffocating grip of guilt, remember that there is a way to untangle yourself from its clutches. It's during these moments that you should summon the power of recollection—reflect on those instances when you've managed to find solace amidst the storm of emotions. As you embark on this journey of introspection, consider documenting these moments by writing them down. By capturing them on paper, you're creating a reservoir of reassurance that can be drawn upon whenever the waves of guilt threaten to engulf you once more.

Imagine having a repository of your own past wisdom, a collection of the thoughts that brought you comfort, clarity, and peace. These words, preserved through your writing, become a lifeline—an anchor that steadies you in times of turbulence. It's a tangible reminder that you possess the tools to push through even the most complex emotions, including guilt.

So, whether you're huddled in the quiet of your room or surrounded by the hustle and bustle of life, take a moment to remember. Remember the instances when you managed to calm the storm within, when you were able to see through the haze of guilt to the core of understanding. Write down these instances, no matter how insignificant they might seem at the time. For in the process of documenting them, you're cultivating a garden of resilience, nurturing the seeds of self-compassion and insight.

In our journey toward self-improvement, these moments of solace and clarity serve as guideposts, illuminating the path through the dense forest of guilt. And as you continue to add to this collection, you're arming yourself with a persuasive tool—one that can dispel the darkness of guilt with the light of past wisdom. So as you stand at the crossroads of emotion, take out your pen, open your notebook, and inscribe these precious instances. For in the act of writing, you're not just capturing the past; you're fortifying your present and empowering your future.

CHAPTER 11

STAY IN YOUR LANE

*Combat Jealousy by Recognizing
Your Distinct Playing Field*

There's a joke where a man visits a relative in a mental institution. On the third floor, he hears someone sobbing, "Rachael, Rachael, Rachael." Curious, he enters the room and asks the person about this Rachael. The person explains that he had wanted to marry a woman named Rachael Levine, but she declined his proposals. His mental state deteriorated after that rejection.

The visitor then moves to the fifth floor, where he again hears someone crying "Rachael, Rachael, Rachael." Intrigued by the recurring mention of Rachael, he enters the room and inquires about the situation. The person responds, "Well, I married her, and that's why I'm here."

This joke holds great power in offering a different perspective. When we view everything from within our own shoes and stay within the confines of our own lives, we risk experiencing intense jealousy as we look at the external lives of others. Jealousy is a powerful force.

It has the power to upend lives, ruin relationships, and build resentment. Taking a closer look at jealousy prompts the realization that we are each navigating our distinct playing field, marked by individual strengths and tribulations. Understanding that we are in our own lane allows us to appreciate our unique journey, prompting us to play to our strengths and cultivate a sense of fulfillment within our own narrative rather than succumbing to the comparison trap. This transformative mindset not only dismantles the toxic roots of jealousy but also propels us toward embracing the richness of our own path and celebrating the diverse journeys of those around us.

Remember that Perceptions Can Be Deceiving

Interestingly, a couple once confessed their envy of their seemingly serene neighbors, who appeared to have a quiet and peaceful home. In contrast, the couple's own household was often filled with noise due to frequent fights and arguments. Little did they realize that the neighbors' tranquility stemmed from a lack of communication between them for years. They literally didn't talk at all to each other. This serves as a powerful reminder that perceptions can be deceiving.

The lens through which we view the lives of others can often be distorted by the filters of our own perceptions. It's a common human tendency to romanticize the experiences of those around us, assuming that their lives are free from the challenges and difficulties we ourselves face. The danger lies in the deceptive allure of our fictionalized perceptions, leading us down the treacherous path of envy and discontent. We must challenge these idealized perceptions and recognize that everyone, irrespective of appearances, grapples with their unique set of challenges and adversities. By acknowledging the universality of struggles, we cultivate a more empathetic and grounded perspective, establishing a sense of connection rather than comparison.

Jealousy often stems from an incomplete understanding of the complexities of others' lives. It's essential to actively challenge the assumptions we make about the ease and perfection we perceive in the lives of those around us. Reminding ourselves that every individual is navigating their own path, replete with highs and lows, helps dismantle the misconception of a perfect existence. Embracing the reality that challenges are inherent in the human experience allows us to shift from a mindset of comparison to one of empathy, fostering a more compassionate approach to ourselves and others.

Recognize the Struggle behind the Success

Few emotions wield the power and complexity of jealousy. It's a familiar specter that often tiptoes into our lives, armed with comparisons and fueled by the yearning for what others seem to possess. Is there a singular thread that can, with gentle precision, undo the knots of envy? A tale unfolds, one of self-discovery, fleeting epiphanies, and the often-neglected art of forgetting—forging a narrative that has the potential to liberate.

In a modest gathering of minds and conversations, I once found myself in the company of an individual who bore the weight of envy within his heart. It was a form of envy that had dug its talons deep into his psyche, triggered by the success of none other than his own brother-in-law. The brother-in-law's trajectory through the field of business had been nothing short of impressive, laden with achievements that sparkled like gems on a crown. However, this observer of success, this individual, held a firm belief—an unwavering conviction—that the accomplishments adorning his brother-in-law's life were not the fruits of merit or hard work but chance occurrences, fortunate accidents borne out of luck.

Within this frame of perception, his own aspirations seemed to dim in the radiant glow of his brother-in-law's achievements. As he shared his feelings, a narrative unfurled—a tale steeped in a mixture of yearning and resentment. His personal milestones, which had once gleamed as beacons of progress, now appeared minimized, muted under the looming shadow of his brother-in-law's triumphs. Every glance at his brother-in-law's opulent house or luxurious car sparked a quiet ember of resentment, a reminder of his own perceived lack of fortune.

And yet, within the ebb and flow of dialogue, a question emerged, carrying with it a subtle weight that belied its simplicity: "Is there a moment when you thought about your brother-in-law's success without the overpowering shroud of jealousy?" It was a question posed not merely to elicit a response but to act as a chisel, delicately carving through layers of envy to uncover the essence of understanding that might lie beneath.

At first, the jealous man's memory seemed an impenetrable fortress, guarded by the sentinels of resentment. The jealousy that seemed to invade every thought had obscured the possibility of any memory that didn't bear the stain of envy. Yet, through the persistent rhythm of conversation, an ember of recollection was unearthed—a memory that had long been overshadowed, dormant beneath the weight of his emotions.

This memory, like an artifact from a distant time, beckoned to be brought into the light. It was a memory that hearkened back to a day when he had stepped into the bustling heart of his brother-in-law's office—a realm alive with the heartbeat of victories and challenges. In that singular visit, he had glimpsed, beyond the surface, a narrative that wasn't limited to glossy accomplishments but rather a symphony of efforts and tribulations that often played in the background. As he shared this memory, he described, with vivid detail, how he had witnessed firsthand the weight of responsibility that his brother-in-law bore upon his shoulders. It wasn't a rosy picture of uninterrupted success that he had beheld; it was a canvas painted with the hues of resilience, of challenges bravely faced, and of victories hard-won.

The jealous man narrated the stories from his brother-in-law's company that often went untold, the deals that had seemed all but sealed, only to unravel in the face of unforeseen rejections. He was there when a costly misstep by a worker threatened to dismantle the foundation of a significant account, a misstep that spoke volumes about the fragile nature of success. But this was merely the beginning of the narrative that unfolded before him. Beyond these moments, a more intricate picture came into focus. He stood as an observer as one of his brother-in-law's partners stormed into the office, his voice carrying the echoes of frustration and anger. He listened as the symphony of success was interwoven with the cadence of customer complaints— complaints that served as reminders that even amidst triumph, the journey was not without its hurdles. An investor's inquiry into the sluggish progress of an investment offered a stark reminder that challenges could arise even in the midst of success.

It was in these moments that the fortress of envy began to crumble. The carefully constructed narrative—that success was solely the result of fortunate happenstance—revealed its fragile nature. An understanding emerged, akin to a fledgling bud pushing through the cracks in concrete. The realization that success, even in its most dazzling forms, wasn't merely luck, but rather the product of tireless effort, sleepless nights, and a relentless determination, began to take root.

With this newfound understanding, his perception of his brother-in-law's journey underwent a transformation. The gloss of luck, once attributed to the achievements, faded away, giving rise to an image of a man who had charted his course through stormy waters. The car, once a symbol of material prosperity, took on a deeper significance—a symbol of the sacrifices, resilience, and hard-won battles that lay hidden beneath the surface.

And yet, in this narrative, a layer of irony is unveiled—a twist that reminds us of the transient nature of epiphanies. He confessed that this revelation was ephemeral. The memory that had once offered a window into a different perspective slowly faded, like a star whose brilliance waned as dawn approached. The allure of envy, like a siren's call, drew him back into its embrace.

As the memory of that visit and the insights it had birthed retreated into the recesses of his mind, he returned to the fold of his original belief—the belief that his brother-in-law's accomplishments were rooted solely in luck. Each time his gaze fell upon the luxurious car, envy surged anew, washing away the sands of understanding he had momentarily grasped. It was as if the sands of time had conspired to bury the treasure he had uncovered, leaving behind only a trace of its presence.

This tale of oscillation—of a pendulum that swings between comprehension and envy—unveils a truth that resonates deeply within the chambers of human experience. It underscores the fluid nature of perception, a reminder that understanding and insight can sometimes be as fleeting as a passing breeze, obscured once again by the storm clouds of envy.

Yet, within this dance of emotions and realizations, there exists a lesson—a lesson that finds a resonant echo with the very theme that underpins this narrative. It is a lesson that speaks to the human tendency to forget our own thoughts that once offered solace. The memory of that moment when the fortress of jealousy trembled, when the façade of luck crumbled, was not lost due to insignificance. It wasn't a mere footnote in the chronicle of emotions. Rather, it was overshadowed by the magnetic pull of old habits, the gravitational force of envy that threatened to reclaim its throne.

In an effort to anchor his shifting thoughts and confront his jealous sentiments, I encouraged him to pen down this statement: "My brother-in-law richly deserves his success. His unwavering effort, sleepless nights, and relentless battle with stress have paved the path to his current achievements—not mere luck." I suggested that he take up this ritual, inscribing these words daily upon the canvas of his thoughts until they became an indelible part of his mental landscape. This practice, I hoped, would serve as a gentle reminder of the perspective that had once calmed his storm of envy, steering him toward a more balanced understanding of his brother-in-law's journey.

As you traverse the vast landscapes of your emotions, let this story be your guide. Let it be a reminder that envy can sometimes obscure the very insights that have the power to liberate us from its clutches. When thoughts of jealousy entwine themselves around your heart, when comparisons and yearnings cloud your vision, take a pause—a moment of introspection. Reflect on whether, in the midst of your envy, there was ever a flicker of understanding or a fragment of thought that recognized that someone's success isn't solely a product of luck. Consider if, even for a fleeting instant, you marveled at their achievements not as the result of cosmic fortune but as the culmination of sweat, tears, and unwavering determination. Recall if you ever saw beyond the gleam of success, to the stories of setbacks, rejections, and sleepless nights that often remained untold.

In the hush of that moment, you might unearth the key to your own liberation—a key that unlocks the door from envy to respect, from comparison to celebration. For within the folds of our human experiences lies the potential to break free from the shackles of jealousy, to forge connections with the stories that reside beneath the surface, and to remember the thoughts that, at least once, served as lighthouses in the storm.

This narrative, this tale of a journey from jealousy to fleeting understanding and back again, is a mirror to the human condition. It holds up a reflection of our own tendencies, our capacity for both enlightenment and forgetfulness. It underscores the fact that the journey to transformation, to transcending envy, is not linear but rather a dance—a dance between the forces that pull us toward jealousy and the insights that push us toward understanding.

Let this story be a reminder that just as the tides rise and fall so do our emotions. The next time jealousy's shadows loom large, remember that there was a moment when understanding shone through. Remember that you once saw the effort behind the achievements, the struggle behind the success.

Appreciate the Distinct Journeys of Others

In the heart of a bustling city, there lived two childhood friends, Alex and George. Growing up in the same neighborhood, their lives took divergent paths as they entered adulthood. George, a talented artist with a deep passion for painting, struggled to make ends meet. Alex, on the other hand, found himself riding the waves of success as a tech entrepreneur.

As years passed, envy began to take root in George's heart. Every glance at his friend's opulent lifestyle, complete with a sleek penthouse and luxury cars, ignited a burning ember of resentment. He couldn't fathom why he, a gifted artist, had to endure financial struggles while Alex seemed to be showered with blessings.

One day, George confronted his feelings head-on. Sitting in front of his easel, he decided to paint a portrait of his friend Alex—a portrait that would capture the essence of his life. As he painted, George found himself diving into memories, reflecting on the path both he and Alex had taken.

As the painting took shape, George's resentment transformed into understanding. He depicted Alex in his penthouse, surrounded by state-of-the-art gadgets and stylish furniture. But alongside the glossy exterior, George added layers of complexity. He painted the countless hours Alex spent buried in work, the sleepless nights agonizing over strategies and dealing with the challenges of running a business.

Next, George painted a scene of Alex's luxurious car. However, the canvas revealed not just the car's gleaming surface but also the stresses and pressures it concealed. George depicted the late-night phone calls with clients in different time zones, the tense negotiations with investors, and the weight of responsibilities that accompanied success.

As George continued to paint, a revelation dawned upon him. The luxurious life he had once envied wasn't simply a result of luck. It was a culmination of relentless effort, sleepless nights, and an unwavering commitment to overcoming challenges. He realized that while he had chosen the path of art, Alex had embarked on a journey filled with its own struggles and sacrifices.

Completing the painting, George stepped back to admire his creation. The canvas now told a story—a story of the effort behind Alex's success, a story that showcased the intricate threads woven into the fabric of his achievements. The painting was no longer just an image; it was a mirror that reflected George's own journey, his own struggles, and his own choice of artistic expression.

With newfound clarity, George hung the painting in his studio, a constant reminder that success wasn't solely a result of luck. He wrote down the words he had painted—words that echoed the sentiment that his friend's accomplishments were hard-earned. Each day, as he looked at the painting and repeated those words, he found solace in the understanding that everyone's journey was unique, shaped by their choices and efforts.

Over time, George's envy transformed into admiration. He realized that success came in various forms, each accompanied by its own set of challenges. The painting became a beacon of empathy, reminding him to celebrate his friend's accomplishments while also embracing his own path. And in this simple act of artistic expression, George found not just a way to conquer jealousy but a way to honor his own journey and the journeys of those around him. As George stood before his masterpiece, he recognized the power of perspective and understanding. It wasn't just a lesson for him; it was a universal truth that held the potential to liberate anyone ensnared by the clutches of jealousy.

Whether you're standing before a canvas, typing words onto a page, or simply contemplating life's twists and turns, remember that this revelation isn't meant to be confined to one person's story. It's a light that can guide us all. Just as George transformed his resentment into a masterpiece of understanding, you too can rewrite the narrative of your journey. In that moment of remembrance, you might find the strength to break free from the cycle of envy and, in doing so, rewrite the narrative of your own journey.

Inscribed upon the canvas of your thoughts, etched into the parchment of your heart, write down the words that illuminate the path from envy to insight. Commit them to memory, repeat them daily until they become an integral part of your mental landscape. Let these words be a touchstone, a reminder that success isn't solely luck—it's forged through effort, resilience, and dedication.

In this act of writing, in this act of remembrance, you're not just acknowledging the journey of others—you're also affirming your own worth and agency. By recognizing the stories behind success, you're rewriting the story of your own journey. So take up the pen, embrace the brush, or let your fingers dance upon the keyboard, and let these words echo through your thoughts. For in this echo, you'll discover the strength to shatter the chains of envy. You'll find the courage to see beyond the surface, to recognize the threads of effort that weave the fabric of achievements. And as you do, you'll find yourself on a transformative journey, one that leads you from comparison to celebration, from resentment to understanding.

PART 3

ENRICH
YOUR
RELATIONSHIPS

CHAPTER 12

SEEK TO UNDERSTAND OTHERS' EXPERIENCES

Approach Conversations with Empathy

In today's world, many people wonder why divorce rates have skyrocketed. My response is that modern society has bred a culture of zero tolerance, where few are willing to invest the effort needed to sustain relationships. We've become accustomed to instant gratification—think instant coffee and other conveniences. In the past, things weren't so easy. When a refrigerator malfunctioned, we'd diligently attempt to repair it. Contrast that with today's throwaway mentality: if a fridge breaks down, we often discard it and buy a new one. Relationships, like appliances of yesteryears, require patience, care, and maintenance. Just as we once labored to fix our possessions, we must work to mend and nurture our connections with others. This shift in attitude is essential if we're to reverse the trend of disposable relationships and build lasting unions. This section will explore ways we can not only sustain our relationships but also enrich them.

Approaching conversations with empathy is a transformative practice that opens doors to deeper understanding and connection. Recognizing that we don't always know the intricacies of another person's experiences, taking a moment to step into their shoes becomes a crucial aspect of meaningful communication. It's a humble acknowledgment that each individual carries a unique set of challenges, triumphs, and emotions. By actively listening and seeking to understand the world from their perspective, we create a space for genuine connection. Asking about their experiences not only demonstrates a genuine interest but also showcases a willingness to engage with the depth of their narrative. This empathetic approach establishes an environment of trust and openness, laying the foundation for relationships to flourish.

Conversely, entering discussions solely with our own perspective and experiences limits the richness of our interactions. It confines us to the narrow scope of our understanding, hindering the potential for true connection. Empathy, on the other hand, allows us to transcend our preconceived notions and biases. It encourages us to listen with an open heart and mind, creating a space where diverse perspectives can coexist. By embracing empathy in conversations, we not only deepen our relationships but also enrich our own lives by broadening our understanding of the diverse human experience. It becomes a powerful tool for personal growth and societal harmony, reminding us that the tapestry of humanity is woven with threads of shared understanding and compassion.

Invite Others' Perspectives

In my early twenties, I reconnected with a friend from elementary school. It had been quite a while since I had seen him, so I took the opportunity to ask him how he was doing. As our conversation unfolded, it became evident that he was in a state of distress. Our close bond from school gave me the confidence to broach the topic with him. I mentioned that I sensed something was troubling him and offered my assistance if there was anything I could do.

He confided in me, revealing that he was going through an exceptionally challenging period. His mother was grappling with unfortunate mental health issues, and her behavior was taking a toll on him and his siblings. The crux of the matter was that his mother couldn't seem to let her married children live their lives in peace. Instead, she continually harassed them, casting a shadow over their lives. The situation had become increasingly untenable.

As I probed further, he recounted an incident that encapsulated the turmoil they were enduring. Whenever he or his siblings went on vacation, his mother would call them and unleash a torrent of reproach. She'd berate them for embarking on expensive trips they ostensibly couldn't afford. It was evident that my friend and his siblings had reached a breaking point. The weight of the situation was causing them to contemplate severing ties with their own mother—an agonizing decision that no child should ever have to face.

I found myself grappling with this dichotomy—how could a mother object to her children seeking joy and leisure? Although there were complex mental health struggles at play, it still seemed counterintuitive for a parent to object to their children's well-deserved happiness. Could there be a deeper reason behind her seemingly irrational behavior? I shared my thoughts with my friend, suggesting that perhaps his mother was yearning to be heard and valued. It was possible that her antagonistic behavior was a desperate plea for attention and recognition.

I proposed an experiment rooted in empathy and communication. I suggested that the next time he planned a vacation, he could take a bold step. Instead of making the decision in isolation, he could include his mother in the conversation. By inviting her opinion and seeking her advice on the matter, he might provide her with a platform to express herself. This approach could potentially bridge the gap between their perspectives.

My friend hesitated but agreed to give it a shot. He mustered the courage to ask his mother for her input on his vacation plans. It was an exercise in vulnerability, a conscious decision to listen before making a choice. To his astonishment, his mother's response was nothing short of a revelation. Not only did she not oppose the idea of him going on vacation, but she also encouraged it. She acknowledged his hard work and suggested he take a well-deserved break.

In an unforeseen twist, she even went the extra mile by recommending destinations for his vacation. It was a moment of connection—one that shattered preconceived notions and fostered a new level of understanding. My friend's courage to step outside his comfort zone and embrace empathy had paid off in ways he couldn't have imagined.

Months later, I received a phone call from my friend. His voice brimmed with excitement as he recounted the turn of events. The technique I had suggested, born from a simple desire to bridge a communication gap, had transformed his relationship with his mother. He expressed his disbelief that by extending an olive branch and valuing her opinion, he had managed to uncover a new dimension to their bond. Not only had their conversations become more open and candid, but he also felt a newfound closeness to his mother.

In reflecting on this journey, I couldn't help but marvel at the power of empathy, active listening, and understanding. Often, in our quest for resolution and harmony, we overlook the significance of validating someone's feelings and opinions. My friend's experience taught me that even in the face of seemingly insurmountable disagreements, there exists a path toward reconciliation—one that involves acknowledging the other person's perspective and demonstrating that their voice matters.

My friend's struggle with his mother's distressing behavior highlights the transformative potential of empathy. By inviting open communication, embracing vulnerability, and seeking to understand, we can unravel the complexities of human relationships. It serves as a testament to the enduring power of compassion and the remarkable outcomes that arise when we choose to listen and value each other's viewpoints.

Seek a Deeper Understanding of Other's Experiences

Picture a scenario where a father embarks on a bus journey accompanied by his lively and spirited children. These young souls, brimming with vitality and exuberance, exhibit a zest for life that radiates in their carefree actions. They dart around the bus, their laughter echoing through the air, seemingly oblivious to the world around them. Yet, their unrestrained merriment clashes with the serene ambiance desired by the other passengers, including an elderly man who finds himself growing increasingly agitated.

As time passes, the elderly passenger's initial patience wears thin, worn away by the continued exuberance of the children. Their exuberance, once endearing, now begins to irk him. His annoyance escalates into a palpable frustration, prompting him to approach the father with a mix of sternness and irritation. He expresses his displeasure, casting judgment upon the father for what he perceives as a failure to rein in his children's exuberance. The father, no stranger to his parental responsibilities, openly admits his attempts to curb their enthusiasm, though he acknowledges he has had limited success.

Amid the tension that brews between them, the father commits to making further efforts to manage his children's behavior. Yet, despite his genuine determination, his attempts prove to be in vain. The children's boundless energy and youthful zest continue to defy restraint, leading to escalating frustration for both the father and the increasingly vexed elderly passenger.

In a subsequent encounter, the elderly man's patience erodes entirely. He approaches the father once again, his exasperation evident, and delivers an ultimatum. He implores the father to exert control over his children, warning that if this proves impossible, he himself will intervene—with potentially unpleasant consequences. The father, maintaining an air of sincerity, acknowledges his shortcomings and the inherent challenges of maintaining order in such circumstances. Nevertheless, he assures the older man that he is resolute in his commitment to rectify the situation.

Yet, amidst these exchanges fraught with tension, an unexpected revelation emerges, fundamentally altering the narrative's trajectory.

The father unveils the truth concealed beneath the surface of his children's unruly behavior, exposing the depths of their pain. He discloses that their purpose for embarking on this bus journey is to bid a final farewell to their ailing mother, to see her one last time before her impending departure from this world. The imminent loss of their mother has cast a shadow of confusion and sorrow over their young hearts, rendering them unable to process their emotions in a conventional manner.

With this revelation, a shift occurs—a shift in perspective that reverberates through both the father and the elderly man. The older man's initial frustration evolves into empathetic understanding as he grasps the gravity of the situation. He recognizes the family's emotional turmoil and realizes that the children's apparent unruliness merely masks their internal struggle.

Armed with this newfound understanding, the older man undergoes a remarkable transformation. Rather than reproaching the children, he seeks to connect with them on a deeply human level. He chooses to lend them an empathetic ear, offering a supportive shoulder and a compassionate heart. Engaging with the children, he participates in their games, sharing stories that aim to provide them comfort and solace. He goes a step further, extending a gesture of kindness by offering them a small amount of money—a symbolic token of goodwill.

As the interaction deepens, the eldest child, previously the embodiment of exuberance, finds himself opening up about his feelings. His voice, once animated, now takes on a subdued tone as he begins to articulate the great love he holds for his ailing mother. He expresses the impending void her absence will create in their lives, his eyes brimming with unshed tears. Suddenly, his stoic facade crumbles, and he surrenders to his emotions, his tears flowing freely as he grapples with an overwhelming torrent of feelings.

Remarkably, the older man, who was initially positioned as an adversary, now stands united with the children in their shared vulnerability. As he witnesses the raw pain emanating from the child's soul, he himself becomes emotionally moved. He realizes that beneath the facade presented to the world lies a complex assortment of experiences and emotions, often concealed from casual observers. He comprehends that human actions are rarely straightforward, and a deeper understanding can lead to great transformation.

Thus, as the bus continues its journey, an unexpected metamorphosis unfolds—a metamorphosis that touches every passenger on board. Those who were once perturbed by the children's actions now find themselves wiping away tears from their eyes. The initial anger has metamorphosed into empathy, and the demand for patience has blossomed into a collective recognition of the fragility inherent in human emotions.

This story stands as a testament to the formidable force of empathy and the intrinsic value of reserving judgment. It encourages us to approach others with curiosity and an open heart, acknowledging that beneath every action lies a multifaceted story. It underscores the significance of extending compassion, even in moments of frustration, as we can never fully fathom the battles others wage within themselves. You never know what a person goes through, and yes, you don't always know what your own spouse goes through.

In a world often characterized by hurried judgments and fleeting encounters, this narrative implores us to pause, reflect, and endeavor to comprehend the narratives that shape those around us. It serves as a reminder of the interconnectedness of human experiences, showcasing the resilience and compassion that can be woven into the fabric of daily interactions. Before yielding to anger or annoyance, let us remember that every person carries a story, and their actions may be just one fragment of a much larger whole.

Express Understanding

I once had an experience while traveling to a distant place that left a lasting impression on me. Upon arriving at the airport, I encountered a TSA agent who seemed unusually frustrated and was loudly expressing his discontent. He appeared to be on the verge of losing control, and I couldn't comprehend why he was reacting so intensely. My initial reaction was to respond with sarcasm, perhaps suggesting that he deserved a raise for his passionate dedication. However, I quickly reconsidered and tried to put myself in his shoes.

Recalling the wise words of my father, a respected authority in mental health within the Orthodox Jewish community, I reminded myself not to judge people too quickly. My father's counsel had always guided me to remember that we never truly know the challenges and struggles someone might be facing in their life.

Empathy took over, and I decided to approach the situation from a different angle. I told the agent, "I can only imagine how challenging it must be to interact with countless people every day. If I were in your position, I'm not sure I could handle it as well as you do." As I uttered those words, I noticed a transformation in his demeanor. His voice softened, and a single tear rolled down his cheek. He said, "You have no idea how much this means to me. It's the first time in my life that I feel understood."

In that moment, it became clear to me that this individual, who had been projecting frustration and anger, was actually carrying a heavy burden of his own. He had likely endured years of feeling misunderstood and facing his own struggles. I realized the significance of my choice in that interaction. By showing empathy and acknowledging his challenges, I had offered a small dose of understanding that he desperately needed.

Reflecting on the experience, I recognized that choosing empathy over sarcasm had a deep impact. This TSA agent's emotional response was a testament to the power of acknowledging someone's struggles, even in brief encounters. I felt a sense of fulfillment knowing that I had chosen a path that didn't add to his burdens, but instead provided a moment of genuine connection.

This encounter reminded me of the depth and complexity that each person carries within. It reinforced the importance of approaching others with empathy and kindness, as we can never truly fathom the battles they may be fighting. It also illustrated how a simple shift in perspective can transform an interaction from one of frustration to one of understanding and connection.

I recently had a similar experience when I had a conversation with the CEO of a huge company. Initially, I was taken aback by his rude behavior, and my instinct was to confront him and express my displeasure. However, I decided to take a different approach.

Rather than confronting him, I calmly said, "I've heard from everyone I've spoken to that you're known for your kindness and respectfulness. I can only imagine the weight of the responsibilities you carry as a CEO, especially on tough days." He seemed surprised by my response and began to open up about the immense pressure he faces daily, compounded by the challenges of a loved one's serious illness.

Expressing empathy, I remarked, "Dealing with such pressures requires incredible strength. I'm genuinely amazed by your resilience." As our conversation continued, we developed a deeper connection, and I realized that my understanding approach had built the foundation for a genuine friendship. From that point on, our relationship has brought me numerous benefits and insights.

This encounter reminded me that sometimes, showing empathy and understanding can lead to unexpected positive outcomes, even in professional settings. When we approach difficult people or conversations with the peace offering of empathy and understanding, it can truly disarm hostility and open the floor for genuine connection and a very human moment. Consider times when someone approached you with empathy and extended understanding even when you were having a bad day or feeling unappreciated. How did their words land for you? How did you respond to them?

Through looking back and getting in touch with times when you felt understood, you are better equipped to approach anyone in any and every situation. You don't have to have gone through what other people are going through to understand how much it means for someone to stop and see you clearly.

A person once asked their rabbi, "Why do we have two ears but only one mouth?" The rabbi's reply is insightful: "So we can listen twice as much as we speak." This anecdote illustrates the value of understanding and empathetic listening in relationships. It's easy to get caught up in our own feelings and perceptions, but taking the time to truly listen to our partner's perspective can lead to a healthier, more harmonious connection.

CHAPTER 13

TAKE RESPONSIBILITY

*Resolve Conflict by Acknowledging
and Owning Your Actions*

There's a famous joke where a person visits a zoo and notices his friend sticking out her tongue at a snake. Perplexed, he inquires, "What's happening here?" His friend responds, "The snake started it! I have plenty of witnesses who saw the snake sticking out its tongue first." This humorous tale highlights the tendency for people to justify their actions by shifting blame onto someone or something else. It reflects the common human inclination to seek validation for our actions, even in situations where it might seem irrational. This concept resonates in relationships too, as partners sometimes find themselves in arguments where both parties claim the other initiated the conflict.

Do you often find yourself caught in frequent arguments with your partner? During those challenging moments, seeking advice to mend the conflict might be your first instinct. Interestingly, the solution might be closer than you think. Reflect on times when you said,

"You have a point," to your partner. Surprisingly, using this simple phrase has the power to initiate a remarkable change: tensions ease, and a harmonious atmosphere returns. What's even more intriguing is that you've employed this technique effectively in the past, even as recently as yesterday. It's curious how this approach slipped your mind today.

Taking responsibility for your actions in the midst of conflict involves acknowledging your partner's standpoint, and this acknowledgment can pave the way for resolution. As you navigate disagreements, don't overlook your own tried-and-true approach—a direct acknowledgment of your partner's viewpoint can serve as the catalyst to restore equilibrium and develop a deeper understanding in your relationship.

Take Responsibility for Your Issues

I once had a man come to see me seeking advice about a recurring issue in his marriage. He shared that he and his wife were constantly bickering, even over seemingly trivial matters. One instance he mentioned was their ongoing disagreement about the air conditioner—he preferred to keep it on because he felt hot, while his wife wanted it off as she felt cold. Sensing there might be more to uncover, I decided to delve deeper into the dynamics of their relationship.

I began by asking the husband a pivotal question: when was the last time he had bought his wife a gift? He recounted that a few months back, he had splurged on an expensive gift for her. I then inquired about his dedication to his work: was he diligently working hard to earn a living? He confirmed that he indeed put in a great deal of effort at work, with the primary goal of ensuring his wife's happiness. With this information, I led him to a realization.

I pointed out that his actions already demonstrated his willingness to make sacrifices for his wife's happiness. The gift he had given her was a testament to his commitment. So, I questioned him further: if he was ready to invest so much in her happiness, why then did he engage in trivial conflicts that required much less effort, such as adjusting the air conditioner? He seemed puzzled by the connection.

I helped him understand that the difference lay in the way his gestures were received. Buying an extravagant gift was a tangible expression of his devotion—a gesture his wife could clearly appreciate. On the other hand, turning off the air conditioner might even be a sacrifice for him, but it didn't convey the same level of thoughtfulness. It lacked the bravado of a meaningful gesture of devotion. The missing element was that his sacrifice of turning off the air conditioner will not convey his love and care for her like a gift would do, so what's the worth of sacrificing?

With this realization, I offered a solution: next time he found himself in a similar situation, he should communicate his willingness to make a sacrifice in a way that mirrored the sentiment behind a thoughtful gift. I suggested he say something like, "You know, I'm really feeling hot, but because I love you so much, I can't bear to see you uncomfortable." By framing his concession as an expression of his love and care, he could tap into the same motivation that drove him to buy gifts for her.

Two weeks later, I unexpectedly bumped into the husband. He had a smile on his face as he recounted a new twist in their interactions.

This time, they were engaged in a different kind of disagreement. He shared that his wife wanted the air conditioner on to ensure his comfort, while he wanted it off to make her feel comfortable. Chuckling, I congratulated him—it seemed they had progressed from quarreling over petty matters to a more heartwarming kind of dispute.

As I was reflecting on the story I just shared, it reminded me of another tale I once relayed to a couple. In this couple, each partner seemed to focus solely on the other's areas for improvement, often neglecting their own shortcomings. In fact, one spouse took it a step further and projected his own issues onto his partner, blaming her for the very same problem he struggled with. Seeing how worked up he was when he told me this, I decided that this moment was not the right time and place to point out his projection. Instead, I chose to drive the point home with a humorous story, hoping it would make him more aware.

The story unfolds like this: a husband walked into a pharmacy and explained that his wife had severe hearing issues and needed hearing aids as a gift. The pharmacy staff suggested he test the extent of her hearing loss first. They advised him to stand on the second floor, ask her what was for supper, and continue moving closer to her until she responded. This way, he could gauge the severity of her impairment.

The husband returned home and initiated the test. "Ann, what's for supper today?" he shouted from the second floor. No answer. He proceeded downstairs and repeated the question, "Ann, what's for supper today?" Still no response. He got even closer, "Ann, what's for supper today?" Yet she remained silent. The husband began to worry, thinking, "It's even worse than I thought." Finally, he stood in front of her and asked, "Ann, what's for supper today?" She retorted, "I've told you a thousand times already, fried chicken and rice. Your hearing is deteriorating day by day. At first, I thought maybe you couldn't hear me because you were on the second floor, but my goodness, you couldn't even hear me just a few feet away!"

The husband returned to the pharmacy baffled and asked the staff, "How did you know it was me with the hearing problem? How did you politely guide me to realize that I was the one with the issue?" The staff member replied, "It's simple. You kept asking me the same question repeatedly after I'd already answered it. It's not rocket science."

I turned to the husband and pointed out, "It turns out that he was the one with the hearing problem all along, not his wife." The husband burst into laughter, and my message hit home.

The essence of the story resonates in the couple's dynamics. Just as the husband in the story projected his hearing issue onto his wife, this couple was projecting their issues onto each other. It's easier to focus on what others should change than to acknowledge our own areas for growth. By sharing this anecdote, my intention was to help them recognize that sometimes, we might see in others what we don't want to acknowledge within ourselves.

When conflicts arise, it's often a fruitful exercise to take a step back and reflect on the dynamics at play. Are we projecting our own challenges onto others? Are we blaming them for what we may need to address within ourselves? It's a reminder that acknowledging our own vulnerabilities and working on our self-improvement can lead to better understanding and harmony within our relationships.

During my time in high school, I encountered a challenge that tested my self-control. I had always been a diligent student, and my teacher held me in high regard. However, there was a particular incident that stands out. One day, in the midst of the teacher's lecture, a classmate of mine said something that cracked me up. I couldn't hold back my laughter, and my teacher's expression changed from one of authority to one of anger and disappointment.

As the lecture concluded, he unleashed his frustration on me in front of the entire class. His words were sharp and critical, his accusations stung. I found myself on the brink of responding in kind, ready to defend myself and confront him about my innocence. But I paused, reminding myself of the wisdom I had learned from various sources, particularly my parents.

I knew that reacting in anger would only escalate the situation, and I also knew that my teacher's actions were a reflection of his own frustrations. Instead of engaging in a verbal battle, I chose a different path. With a deep breath, I looked at my teacher and said, "I deeply regret my actions. It was thoughtless of me to disrupt your lecture with my laughter, and I am genuinely sorry. I understand the importance of maintaining a respectful learning environment."

The effect of my response was immediate. My teacher's expression shifted from anger to surprise and then to a sense of realization. It was as if my willingness to take responsibility for my actions caught him off guard. He paused for a moment, seemingly taken aback by my composed and sincere apology. And then, unexpectedly, he softened.

"Joel," he said, his tone notably less harsh, "I want to apologize to you as well. I know that you are a diligent student, and I shouldn't have reacted so strongly. You were merely caught off guard by your classmate's remark."

By resisting the urge to engage in a defensive argument, I not only defused a potentially explosive situation but also gained several valuable outcomes. Firstly, I prevented the situation from escalating into a heated confrontation. Secondly, I experienced a sense of pride in my ability to remain composed and handle the situation maturely. And finally, by taking the high road, I prompted my teacher to reflect on his own reaction and acknowledge his overreaction.

This incident served as a reminder that responding with self-control and empathy can yield unexpected positive results. It showed me that by choosing to address a situation with humility and understanding, we not only defuse tension but also create an environment where conflicts can be resolved amicably.

Be Open to Learning

One of my friends, a remarkably successful businessman, once shared his enthusiasm about hiring one of the industry's most esteemed consultants. He insisted that I meet this consultant, and I was genuinely intrigued. Upon our introduction, I was immediately struck by the consultant's evident brilliance. However, as our conversation unfolded, I began to notice a significant flaw in his approach.

It became clear that the consultant faced a considerable challenge: he was unable to pivot away from a strategy even when it became apparent that it was failing. No matter the effort he invested in devising a plan, if it didn't yield the desired results, he would steadfastly double down on it. This rigidity troubled me.

I decided to share my observations with my friend. I acknowledged the consultant's brilliance, but I voiced my concerns about his inability to adapt when faced with the reality that a strategy wasn't working as intended. I expressed doubts about the consultant's capacity to adjust his approach based on the evolving circumstances on the ground.

As a friend, I felt an obligation to highlight this potential flaw, especially considering the substantial salary my friend was investing in the consultant's services. My friend appreciated my candor and valued my opinion, though he respectfully disagreed with my assessment in this particular instance. While he respected my judgment overall, he believed that the consultant's strengths outweighed this potential weakness.

Understanding that differences of opinion are natural, I didn't push the matter further.

I recalled a potent quote from my father: "Unwanted advice is equivalent to criticism."

I figured that time would reveal the accuracy of my observations.

About a month later, my friend reached out to me with unexpected news. He had decided to part ways with the consultant, and he humbly admitted that I had been right all along. The very issue I had raised earlier had become the catalyst for the consultant's dismissal. The consultant's inability to adapt and revise his strategies in response to changing circumstances had indeed become a stumbling block.

Reflecting on this situation, I was reminded that even the brightest minds can falter. Success doesn't solely depend on intellect; it requires a willingness to acknowledge when something isn't working and the flexibility to adjust accordingly. My friend's experience served as a valuable lesson for both of us. It highlighted the importance of adaptability, even for those with exceptional talents.

In the end, the story is a reminder that being open to learning from others, even in moments of disagreement, can lead to better outcomes in the long run. Embracing a mindset that is open to learning from others, even in the face of conflicts, can significantly benefit our relationships, personally and professionally. When we approach disagreements with an open mind, we not only foster a spirit of cooperation but also create opportunities for personal growth. Each interaction becomes a chance to gain insights, broaden perspectives, and cultivate empathy. The willingness to learn from others, even in moments of tension, lays the foundation for stronger, more durable connections. By valuing diverse perspectives and considering alternative viewpoints, we not only approach conflicts more effectively but also cultivate an environment where mutual understanding and respect can thrive.

Hone the Art of Apologizing

When it comes to discussions about relationships, many individuals caught up in disputes understand the potential magic of three simple words: "I am sorry." Yet, intriguingly, they often find themselves hesitating to utter these words. The fear stems from the worry that such an admission might be perceived as a sign of weakness, causing their opponent to hold them in lower regard.

However, it's worth pondering: how many instances in life have you inadvertently wronged someone and, upon genuinely apologizing, not only resolved the issue but also garnered increased respect for your willingness to acknowledge the error?

There seems to be a common tendency for people to assume that admitting mistakes inflicts damage upon their pride. Curiously, reality frequently operates in the opposite manner. Demonstrating the courage to own up to a mistake often showcases emotional strength and maturity. It indicates a willingness to take responsibility for one's actions and to work toward rectifying the situation.

In the end, the ability to say "I am sorry" emerges as a testament to a person's character, illustrating humility and a commitment to maintaining healthy relationships. So, rather than weakening one's stance, the act of apologizing bolsters connections, fosters understanding, and contributes to personal growth.

I used to believe that individuals who couldn't acknowledge their mistakes were driven by overwhelming egos, unable to accept any wrongdoing. However, over the years of interacting with people, I've been surprised to discover that many who struggle to admit errors do so not out of ego but due to a lack of self-esteem. Their self-opinion is so diminished that confessing a mistake would only further cement their sense of being a failure.

On the contrary, those who hold themselves in high esteem approach things differently. They acknowledge that, while they've made numerous sound decisions, accepting an occasional blunder doesn't undermine their overall competence. They understand that admitting a singular misjudgment among a multitude of wise choices is a sign of strength and self-assuredness.

Remember, when faced with an attack, responding with kindness instead of responding in kind will yield much better results. This principle became evident in a story involving a friend of mine who holds a black belt in karate. He once unintentionally cut off another driver while on the road. As the traffic light turned red, my friend noticed the infuriated driver stepping out of his car, his face contorted with anger and his fist raised menacingly. Sensing trouble, my friend calmly emerged from his own car and extended his hand with a warm smile, asking, "How are you, my friend?"

The driver's fury was instantly replaced with bewilderment. He had anticipated a physical confrontation, yet he found himself confronted with a friendly handshake. This unexpected gesture defused the tension and caught the irate driver off guard. My friend sincerely apologized for his mistake, and just like that, the situation was resolved peacefully. What's intriguing is that my friend's choice wasn't based on an inability to defend himself—in fact, with his skills in karate he could have easily subdued his opponent. Instead, he demonstrated the wisdom of understanding that avoiding a fight is a greater victory than winning one.

When we react to aggression with kindness, we disarm hostility and create an opening for understanding. Responding in kind only escalates conflicts, whereas owning our actions and choosing empathy can lead to surprising resolutions. My friend's approach showcases the power of de-escalation, illustrating that steering away from aggression not only diffuses immediate tensions but also earns respect, admiration, and even friendships. It's a reminder that true strength lies not in physical dominance but in the mastery of our own emotions and the ability to transform hostility into harmony.

Reject a Victim Mentality

Throughout my years of working to mend deep and complex conflicts between partners, I've come to realize a crucial factor that can severely damage a relationship: the development of self-pity. When a partner starts feeling unfairly attacked by their significant other without valid reasons, it can lead to a toxic sense of victimhood. This kind of emotional cancer can linger, festering grudges and eroding the foundation of a healthy partnership.

However, there is a way to address this issue. Instead of letting the feelings of victimhood take root, individuals can choose to reflect on the reasons behind their partner's actions. It's important to note that I'm referring to situations within generally healthy relationships, not abusive ones. For instance, if you find yourself being attacked by your partner seemingly out of nowhere, consider whether something you said or did may have unintentionally hurt them before. This perspective shift can help put the attack in context, making it easier to understand that their response might be a reaction to a previous hurtful incident.

By adopting this mindset, partners are less likely to hold onto grudges for extended periods. People naturally seek justification for their experiences, and if they can rationalize why they were attacked, it becomes easier to let go of the resentment. Of course, there are situations where one partner may be going through a personal hardship, which could explain their behavior as well.

In essence, when partners resist the urge to assume the role of the victim and instead seek to understand the motivations behind each other's actions, they pave the way for greater empathy and forgiveness. By embracing this approach, individuals contribute to an environment where conflicts can be resolved more effectively and relationships can thrive.

Find Common Ground

Two highly influential individuals, who were once the closest of friends, found themselves entangled in a bitter dispute. A simple misunderstanding had transformed them from allies to bitter adversaries. Despite the earnest efforts of everyone in the congregation to mediate between them, the rift seemed insurmountable.

In the face of this conflict, I was audacious enough to believe that I could succeed where older, seasoned individuals had failed. Armed with determination and a youthful imagination, I devised a plan. It involved tapping into their individual strengths and unique talents, and exploiting a situation where they couldn't cross-verify my statements.

My strategy commenced with discreetly gathering information from various members of the congregation. I probed into the distinct qualities that person A and person B excelled at—qualities that the other conspicuously lacked. Once I had gathered this information, I approached person A and disclosed that I had spoken with person B. To my advantage, person A remained oblivious to the fact that I had never actually spoken to person B. I shared with person A that person B supposedly told me how he admired his skills, planting seeds of admiration and emulation.

Subsequently, I repeated the same process with person B, weaving a similar narrative. I recounted how person A had spoken highly of person B's unique talents and how person A was envious of these attributes. It was a clever manipulation of information, exploiting the communication gap between them.

As time progressed, the effects of my well-intentioned scheme began to manifest. The two former friends, having been indirectly exposed to one another's perceived admiration and aspiration, found themselves reconsidering their grievances. Slowly but surely, the bitterness started to dissolve. Their egos, initially the driving force behind their discord, were now being channeled toward mutual understanding and camaraderie. Before long, a remarkable transformation occurred. The two influential figures who were once on the brink of irreparable separation were rekindling their friendship. The walls that had been built from misunderstandings and miscommunication began to crumble, giving way to renewed respect and a shared appreciation for each other's talents.

Looking back, my audacious attempt to mend their relationship, fueled by the belief that I could succeed where others had faltered, yielded surprising results. It wasn't a perfect solution, but it taught me the power of perspective and the art of subtle influence. While I may not have been the direct agent of change, I had played a small role in helping them bridge the gap and rediscover the bond they once cherished.

This early experience laid the foundation for my lifelong fascination with human interactions and relationships. It instilled in me the belief that even the most complex conflicts can be alleviated through empathy and an effort to find common ground. Whether you are having a conversation with a stranger or your partner, the goal of finding common ground will set the stage for the relationship. You must understand the other person's perspective and motivations in order to establish this common ground.

I've found that it is all too common for marriage partners and business partners alike to engage in conflicts and eventually start ignoring each other without fully understanding the underlying issues that bother each of them. I recall a situation involving two highly accomplished business partners who jointly managed a multi-million-dollar business. Despite their achievements, they found themselves immersed in a heated dispute. Curious about their perspectives, I requested that they express the other partner's viewpoint before initiating any negotiations. Surprisingly, they exchanged puzzled glances, each one revealing a lack of insight into the other's grievances. Witnessing two accomplished middle-aged individuals struggle to comprehend each other's perspectives was undeniably disconcerting. Only when we approach conversations and relationships with empathy and a desire to understand the other person's perspective will we begin to experience the fruits of our relationships and to build lasting bonds with those around us. Understanding one another's viewpoints is crucial to resolving conflicts effectively.

Respond Rather than React

On one occasion, I attended a gathering where I observed two business partners engaged in a conversation at the end of a table. I was familiar with one of the partners, and I couldn't help but notice how respectfully they were speaking to each other. The one partner was doing the talking while the other partner listened attentively and showed genuine interest. It seemed like a prime example of effective communication between partners.

However, a few days later, I received a call from the partner I knew, and to my surprise, he was seeking my help to mediate a conflict between him and his partner. He explained that their situation had rapidly deteriorated, and I couldn't believe it. I inquired further, wondering how this could happen after witnessing their seemingly harmonious conversation.

He revealed the shocking truth: during that conversation, his partner had issued a threat, stating that if they couldn't reach an agreement, he would run him out of town. I was taken aback, yet I admired the way my acquaintance had handled the situation. I asked him how he managed to remain composed and listen so attentively, despite the threat he had received. His response was both enlightening and remarkable.

He said, "I realized that in this large gathering, there might be others who don't treat their partners with respect. I saw an opportunity to be a positive example of how partners should interact. Nobody knew about the threat; all they saw were two partners treating each other with dignity and respect." I was truly astounded by his selflessness and his ability to rise above the hostility.

This story serves as a powerful reminder that even in the face of adversity, we have the choice to respond with grace and maturity. Instead of reacting to the threat or seeking revenge, he chose to embody the principles he believed in, showing that respectful communication is crucial, even when faced with mistreatment. It's a lesson in holding onto one's values and maintaining a sense of dignity, regardless of the circumstances.

I once received a frantic call from a mother who was irate about her son's situation. It was evident that her anger was rooted in a misunderstanding, and I immediately felt the urgency to rectify the situation. However, as she launched into a tirade, I realized that trying to reason with her while she was in this state would likely be counterproductive.

My initial impulse, like many people's, was to raise my voice to compete with hers and make sure my message got through. Yet I paused and reminded myself of how frequently such attempts escalate conflicts rather than resolve them. Shouting matches seldom lead to mutual understanding; they merely feed into the emotional turmoil.

Reflecting on past experiences, I recalled a strategy I had used in similar situations. Instead of matching volume for volume, I decided to take a different approach. Speaking calmly and softly, I addressed the issue with a measured tone. This had a surprising effect—it created a stark contrast between my composed manner and her escalating anger.

In the heat of the moment, people often become unaware of their own behavior. It's as if they're speeding along at 100 mph, and they don't realize how fast they're going until they encounter something moving more slowly. By using a deliberately quiet voice, I created that contrast for her, making her realize how vehemently she was expressing herself.

As I continued speaking softly, her own voice began to subside. This gradual decrease in volume allowed me to communicate the crucial information that had been obscured by her initial rage. We worked through the misunderstanding, and the situation quickly turned around.

The incident reaffirmed an important lesson: responding with calmness and clarity often trumps responding with intensity. When emotions are running high, attempting to match the other person's energy level can lead to a cycle of heightened emotions. Instead, maintaining composure can serve as a powerful tool to de-escalate conflicts.

In essence, this approach helps people recognize the disparity between their emotional state and the level of their communication. By choosing to stay calm and composed, we can guide the conversation toward a productive resolution. This technique is a subtle yet effective way to restore rational dialogue in the face of anger and miscommunication. Remember, in tense situations, it's not always about how loudly you speak but rather about how thoughtfully you communicate. By staying composed and addressing misunderstandings with a measured tone, you not only diffuse potential conflicts but also create an environment where true understanding can thrive.

The distinction between responding and reacting to a situation holds the key to the dynamics of our relationships. Reacting is often impulsive, driven by immediate emotions and instincts, whereas responding is a thoughtful, measured action guided by consideration and composure. When conflicts arise, maintaining composure and responding thoughtfully allows us to navigate challenges with grace and poise. By taking responsibility for our responses, we not only demonstrate emotional intelligence but also contribute to the cultivation of a positive environment. This approach not only strengthens our relationships but also earns the respect of those who witness our composed and responsible handling of conflicts. It's through these deliberate responses that we shape our interactions and contribute to the overall health and resilience of our connections with others.

When you identify certain subjects that tend to ignite a firestorm of emotions between you and your partner, consider delivering those topics to each other in written form. There are three primary advantages to communicating in writing. Firstly, expressing your thoughts in writing allows for careful consideration and thoughtfulness, ensuring that your partner's feelings are not needlessly hurt. Secondly, the absence of interruptions from your partner guarantees that your message is conveyed in its entirety. Lastly, providing your partner with a written message allows them to read and re-read it multiple times, allowing for a thorough absorption of the content. By opting for written communication in sensitive matters, you are developing a more constructive and effective way of addressing challenging topics within your relationship.

In the realm of relationship conflicts, taking responsibility for one's actions is a linchpin for resolution and growth. Acknowledging and owning up to the role one played in the conflict introduces an element of humility into the conversation, disarming potential hostility and defensiveness. This act of accountability lays the foundation for constructive dialogue so understanding can flourish. When coupled with an empathetic exploration of the other person's perspective, the transformative power of conflict resolution becomes evident. The combination of humility, accountability, and empathy acts as a catalyst, facilitating a quicker and more effective resolution to conflicts, ultimately paving the way for strengthened relationships and personal growth.

CHAPTER 14

SHOW KINDNESS READILY

Connect with People through Showing Up and Being Kind

Sometimes merely showing up for someone can make a huge difference in their lives and help us feel more connected to others. Kindness goes a long way. Whether in times of celebration or moments of struggle, the genuine act of showing up communicates a willingness to share in the joys and burdens of another's journey. This kind of presence goes beyond words; it speaks volumes about the strength of our connections and the depth of our empathy.

Kindness has the capacity to travel great distances and leave an enduring impact. It is the quiet force that bridges the gaps between individuals and cultivates a sense of shared humanity. Acts of kindness, big or small, foster a collective spirit of compassion. In a world that can often feel disconnected, extending kindness becomes a transformative gesture, creating ripples of warmth that resonate within the hearts of both the giver and the receiver. Through simple acts of kindness, we reaffirm our interconnectedness and recognize the truth that kindness is a language that transcends barriers, bringing us closer to one another.

Put Yourself in the Other's Shoes

I was once visiting the opulent offices of a dear friend, who happened to be one of the most generous philanthropists I've ever had the privilege of knowing. This is no small feat in the orthodox Jewish community, where philanthropy holds immense importance. People can boldly approach the doors of influential business figures, even in the midst of their high-stakes transactions, seeking support. These doors swing wide open, and they are often met with the kind of financial assistance that dreams are made of.

During my visit, as I engaged in conversation with my friend, the doorbell rang. A visitor began to spin a tale of dire financial distress. It was evident that this individual was indeed facing financial hardship, but there were astonishing contradictions and embellishments in his story. He seemed to hope that by adding drama and untruths, he could secure a larger contribution. What struck me most was witnessing this brilliant businessman, the revered founder of one of the most esteemed real estate firms, listening with deep empathy. He sighed in solidarity and then, in a grand and magnanimous gesture, presented the visitor with a substantial sum.

I couldn't help but ask my friend how he managed to remain composed and extraordinarily generous in the face of what was clearly a fabricated story. I inquired why he didn't express his skepticism or urge the visitor to be honest without the added embellishments. My friend's response left an indelible mark on me. He said, "Rabbi, put yourself in his shoes. Wouldn't we all try to make our story as dramatic as possible to secure the greatest possible assistance? This individual was undeniably in dire financial straits, and he did his part while I did mine." This response served as a powerful reminder that by endeavoring to understand another person's perspective and truly placing ourselves in their position, not only can we avoid becoming angered, but we can also maintain a deep well of empathy for our fellow human beings.

My friend's act of kindness and his readiness to help this man was inspiring to me. He was able to look past the fabrications of the man's stories and see the real need that existed. The kindness he showed that day encourages me to more readily give what I can and to try to better understand people's motives by putting myself in their shoes.

Do What You Can to Help

I was at the offices of my friend Yossi Gestetner, a brilliant marketing and PR strategist and a prominent figure in the Orthodox Jewish community, engrossed in a strategy session aimed at resolving a significant issue that plagued the community. Amid our brainstorming, Yossi's phone rang, and on the other end was an individual who sounded lost and desperate. He shared a tale of a relative, whom we'll refer to as Andrew, hailing from a broken home, deeply scarred by his upbringing. Falling into the clutches of addiction, Andrew had endured a tumultuous journey. Yet, against all odds, his family rallied, working tirelessly to help him mend his life. Their efforts bore unexpected fruit—he was on the cusp of a date that could potentially lead to an engagement. However, the previous night had taken a troubling turn. A disagreement with friends escalated into a physical altercation. The police were called, and to make matters worse, the local news had caught wind of the incident. They were poised to run a story featuring

Andrew's image, a potential catastrophe that could shatter his progress. The relative implored Yossi to utilize his extensive network of journalist contacts to avert the looming disaster.

Without hesitation, Yossi assured the relative he would do his utmost. He promptly reached out to the journalist responsible for the impending story, sharing the dire predicament that Andrew faced. Yossi conveyed Andrew's journey of struggles and achievements, the pivotal juncture he stood at, and the ruinous consequences the news story could inflict. In his conversation with the journalist, Yossi made a heartfelt plea, proposing that Andrew would enroll in anger management classes to address the issue. The journalist listened attentively, acknowledging the gravity of the situation, but regretfully informed Yossi that the story was already in the final stages of production and would air within the hour.

Undeterred, Yossi was relentless in his pursuit to save Andrew from the looming calamity. He promised the journalist he would call back and then turned to me. Amid the urgency, I found a memory that offered a glimmer of hope—an analogous situation with a course of action that had proven effective. The recollection sparked an idea, and I shared it with Yossi. Yossi, with his exceptional creativity, introduced a highly innovative element to that idea.

Yossi, now fueled by determination, revisited the journalist's plea with renewed conviction. He emphasized the gravity of the situation, highlighting that they were essentially dealing with a matter of life and death. But the journalist, bound by the constraints of the impending broadcast, remained unmoved.

Undaunted, Yossi left no stone unturned, invoking the strategy we had discussed earlier. He reached out to the journalist once more and enacted the plan. Miraculously, the journalist agreed, and the story was halted. The potential catastrophe was averted.

In the aftermath, Andrew's life took a positive trajectory. He committed to anger management classes, got engaged not long after, and now has two beautiful children. Yossi's act of kindness and generosity perhaps altered the course of Andrew's life. He was able to put his past behind him and become the man he wanted to be.

Sometimes simple acts of kindness for people, when we are able to use our talents or resources for their benefit, can be life-changing.

I once received an urgent call—a call that would lead me to an unforgettable encounter. On this fateful day, I received word of an individual in the throes of a severe nervous breakdown. The distressing twist was that this person's agitation had escalated into violence, making their situation even more precarious. Despite the urgency, the individual adamantly refused hospitalization, adding a layer of complexity to the crisis at hand.

The individual's physical strength presented a tangible challenge—one that needed a tactful approach. The collective decision was to explore alternative strategies to convince him to seek medical attention rather than resorting to force. This was when I received a request to intervene, to utilize my skills in communication and empathy to potentially influence this individual's decision.

I recognized the importance of going along with the person's perspective rather than attempting to convince him otherwise. Understanding that battling psychosis with logic is ineffective, I understood the need to approach the situation empathetically and align with his state of mind.

In response, I promptly returned the call from the individual who had reached out to me earlier. My aim was to persuade the distressed person, who had become violent, to consider going to the hospital. I assured the caller that I would arrive on the scene as soon as possible to offer my support and assistance.

Upon arriving at the scene, I observed the person displaying aggressive behavior. Given my physical strength and knowledge of karate techniques, I approached without fear. Addressing him, I asserted, "I am in charge of the emergency personnel, and I won't allow them to take you to the hospital. I don't see any reason for that." This seemed to alleviate his agitation, and he began to open up.

He shared his distress about a neighbor who he believed was intruding on his privacy by tampering with his devices and installing surveillance in his bedroom and bathroom. Expressing empathy, I responded, "That's a terrible situation, and it's completely illegal. We should file a police report and have him arrested for this invasion of your privacy."

Additionally, I informed him of a specialized tool I possessed at home that could identify hidden cameras. I assured him that once we completed the police report and successfully apprehended the individual responsible, I would bring the detector to his residence and eliminate any hidden cameras his neighbor had surreptitiously installed. However, I emphasized that our first priority was initiating the police report and ensuring the arrest of his troublesome neighbor.

I explained that it would be futile to remove the hidden cameras without addressing the root issue. To prevent the neighbor from reinstalling the cameras, it was imperative that he face consequences for his actions. With determination, I conveyed my intention to accompany him to the police station, utilizing my strong connections with law enforcement to ensure that his complaint received the attention it deserved.

I accompanied him in a private car to the hospital rather than using an ambulance. Upon arrival, as we stepped out of the car, he remarked that the surroundings didn't seem like a police station. I explained that in order for the police report to carry weight, we first needed to consult with a specialist who could document the extent of the disruption to his life caused by the neighbor's actions. This specialist would then draft a letter to the police, underscoring the gravity of the situation and urging swift action.

Though he hesitated, he eventually agreed to enter the hospital. He received the necessary treatment, and fortunately, the situation didn't require us to uncover hidden cameras as his fears had suggested. I was able to get him the help he needed, and I was happy to be able to use my gift of mediation to resolve the situation.

Be Present with the Overlooked

I can't resist sharing this joke. Somebody once went to visit his relative in a psychiatric hospital, While in the room with his relative, he overheard a patient in the neighboring room saying, "Could you please come and visit me? I'm feeling so lonely." Feeling sympathetic, the visitor thought, "Why not give this person some human connection?" He entered the room and was surprised to see a man completely naked, except for a beautiful hat atop his head.

Puzzled, the visitor inquired, "Why aren't you dressed?" The patient responded, "I used to get dressed, but then I realized nobody really wants to see me. So, I decided, why bother?" Curious about the hat, the visitor asked, "But why are you wearing that lovely hat?"

The patient replied, "Well, you see, there's always a possibility that someone might come to visit me. So, just in case a kind-hearted soul decides to visit, I've got this fabulous hat on!"

An important part of showing kindness to people is to be with them when they are or feel isolated. There are so many people who are overlooked in our society, and by simply being with those who are often overlooked, we are extending kindness.

I once visited a lonely soul in a nursing home. During that visit, I met a person who seemed weighed down by solitude. With no family to offer companionship, he appeared to be grappling with the pain of isolation. I felt a natural inclination to provide comfort, but to my surprise, he declined. Instead, he confided in me, saying he didn't require comfort. His reason intrigued me, and I pressed him to share.

He hesitated but then revealed his secret: "I'm willing to tell you, but you must promise not to divulge it to anyone in the world." I gave my word, and he began to share his extraordinary belief. He told me that he firmly believed God had chosen him to be the messiah. His conviction was shrouded in secrecy out of fear that any disclosure would jeopardize the divine plan he felt he was a part of. This revelation brought him a sense of purpose and meaning despite his circumstances.

For instance, he explained that even seemingly mundane occurrences like hearing his name called during a televised football game caused him great anxiety. He worried that someone might uncover the reasons behind his name being mentioned and subsequently unravel his role as the messiah. The profound extent of his conviction and the lengths he went to keep it hidden were surprising.

This experience led me to reflect on the complexity of human emotions, beliefs, and the coping mechanisms we create in the face of adversity. The gentleman's conviction might have been a product of his circumstances, but it also served as a source of strength, offering him solace and importance in a world that might have otherwise seemed indifferent to his existence.

I realized that while my initial inclination was to try to persuade him that his beliefs were not grounded in reality, there was a deeper lesson to be learned. The nursing home resident's experience demonstrated the incredible capacity of the human mind to find solace and purpose in the most unexpected places, even in the midst of loneliness and isolation. As a result, I chose not to undermine the person's conviction that he was the messiah. I recognized that even if his belief might seem far from reality, it was providing him with a sense of purpose and significance. This experience taught me that our role as observers and helpers should sometimes extend beyond convincing someone of the objective truth and embrace the delicate balance of respecting their emotions and beliefs, particularly when those beliefs provide them with comfort and meaning.

Sometimes the exercise of just sitting with people and listening to them is a revolutionary act of kindness. It reminds us of our shared humanity and brings moments of connection that are comforting and uplifting for both parties. As we lend an attentive ear, we create a sacred space where thoughts, emotions, and stories can unfold without judgment. Through acts of kindness, we foster a culture of empathy that reminds us of the extraordinary impact of being present for one another in a world that often races by.

CHAPTER 15
EXTEND AUTHENTIC ENCOURAGEMENT

Deepen Bonds through Genuine Words of Appreciation

Authentic encouragement serves as the glue that binds relationships, deepening connections and fostering a sense of mutual appreciation. Expressing genuine praise and appreciation for the qualities, efforts, or achievements of our loved ones creates a positive atmosphere that strengthens the emotional bonds between individuals. When encouragement is sincere and specific, it communicates an understanding of the other person's value and contributions. This mutual upliftment builds a foundation of trust and respect, fortifying relationships against the inevitable challenges life presents.

Even in times of conflict or when expressing criticism, the power of encouragement becomes a bridge toward resolution and understanding. Offering constructive feedback with a spirit of encouragement acknowledges the potential for growth and improvement rather than focusing solely on faults. This approach softens the tension inherent in challenging conversations, allowing individuals to feel supported rather than attacked. By emphasizing shared goals and the belief in each other's capabilities, authentic encouragement becomes a catalyst for healthy conflict resolution, transforming moments of disagreement into opportunities for personal and relational development. In essence, it is the unwavering belief in the potential for positive change that makes encouragement an indispensable tool in navigating the complexities of relationships.

It's invaluable to curate your circle with positivity and encouragement. When you choose companions who radiate optimism, you create an environment where encouragement and inspiration flourish. Even if your close friends mean well, their inherent beliefs can unconsciously influence your perspective, inadvertently dampening your enthusiasm. The power of their convictions can unintentionally seep into your own thoughts, reinforcing doubts or reservations. So aim to surround yourself with those who uplift your aspirations so that together, you can cultivate an atmosphere where dreams can flourish unhindered.

Infuse Praise with Enthusiasm

I recently had a heartfelt interaction with parents who were seeking guidance for their fifteen-year-old child, Jack. They were deeply concerned about his plummeting self-esteem, which left them feeling utterly lost and unsure about how to help him rebuild his sense of self-worth. Their plea for assistance opened the door to an insightful journey of self-discovery and empowerment.

As I listened to their worries, I was struck by their genuine desire to support Jack. They shared that despite their efforts to compliment him, their words seemed to fall flat, leaving Jack unconvinced and unresponsive. He dismissed their compliments as insincere, believing that his parents didn't truly mean what they said. This observation raised an important question: how could they break through this barrier and help Jack regain the confidence he so desperately needed?

To explore this, I suggested involving Jack directly in our conversation. I wanted to establish a connection with him, gain his perspective, and understand the nature of his struggles. When I met Jack, I initiated our dialogue by asking about his interests, friends, and hobbies. It was important for him to feel at ease and to open up to me. By taking a genuine interest in his world, I hoped to create a foundation of trust upon which we could build.

With rapport established, I delved into the heart of the matter. I asked Jack to share his thoughts about what his parents believed about him. His response was candid and revealing: he felt that his parents didn't have much faith in his abilities. He pointed out a glaring discrepancy in their behavior. While they spoke with genuine excitement about the accomplishments of other children, their compliments to him felt lackluster and uninspiring. Jack astutely noted that their words lacked the same enthusiasm, leaving him questioning their authenticity.

As I listened to Jack's perspective, it was clear that he possessed a remarkable level of insight. He wasn't merely dismissing their compliments; he was discerning the emotional tone underlying their words. This led me to a realization: his parents' words were sending an unintended message. Their words, though well-intentioned, were inadvertently reinforcing his perception of inadequacy.

I assured Jack that his feelings were valid and that I understood his perspective. In fact, his ability to discern these subtleties suggested a level of intelligence and self-awareness beyond his years. It was important for him to recognize that his perception was a valuable tool, one that could guide him toward understanding the dynamics of his relationships.

With this understanding in mind, I invited his parents into the conversation to explore their experiences from their point of view. As they shared their thoughts, I inquired about times when Jack had genuinely accepted their compliments. Initially, they struggled to recall any specific instances. Their genuine concern for Jack's well-being was evident as they expressed their desire to see him flourish.

As we continued our discussion, they recounted moments when Jack had indeed accepted their praise. They reflected on what was different during those interactions, attempting to decipher the elusive key to his receptiveness. It became apparent that during those successful instances, their delivery was characterized by increased enthusiasm and authenticity. They remembered that their compliments were not just words; they were infused with genuine excitement and pride.

This revelation brought their journey full circle. Jack's observation that their compliments lacked fervor was echoed in their own discovery. It was a reminder that genuine communication is as much about the emotional intent behind the words as it is about the words themselves. The subtle yet transformative power of enthusiasm in their delivery had ignited a positive response from Jack, even if only on those occasions.

In a final conversation with Jack, I shared the insights that had emerged from our discussions. I encouraged him to reflect on those moments when he did accept their compliments and explore the emotions they evoked. The realization that his parents were indeed capable of genuine pride and enthusiasm became a cornerstone for rebuilding his self-esteem. With this new understanding, Jack was empowered to view their compliments through a different lens.

Before concluding our journey, I shared a larger perspective with his parents. I mentioned that I was in the process of writing a book titled *Rediscover Your Wisdom*. The central theme was that many of the problems people encounter have been faced and solved by them before. Often, we forget our own solutions, and it takes an external trigger to remind us. Their story of uncovering the power of enthusiasm in their communication perfectly encapsulated this concept.

As the weeks passed, the parents reached out to share their joyous news. Jack's transformation had been nothing short of remarkable. With newfound self-assurance, he had embraced his parents' compliments and had flourished. Their commitment to infusing their words with genuine enthusiasm had created a ripple effect of positivity, reigniting Jack's self-esteem and happiness.

This journey was a poignant reminder that seemingly complex problems often have simple solutions, hidden within our own experiences. The key was to listen, reflect, and adapt. Jack's story illustrated the profound impact that small changes in communication could have on a person's self-esteem and well-being. It emphasized the importance of taking a step back and reassessing our approaches, especially when faced with challenges that seem insurmountable. Jack's journey highlighted that even the smallest adjustments in how we communicate and connect with others can yield amazing results.

Let this story serve as a reminder that our interactions, especially with loved ones, hold immeasurable power. The enthusiasm and authenticity we infuse into our words have the potential to uplift and transform lives. By recognizing the weight our communication style carries and learning from our own experiences, we can address the nuances of human relationships with empathy, understanding, and newfound strength.

Express Appreciation Alongside Criticism

I had an individual approach me seeking advice on how to navigate the delicate task of offering constructive criticism to his wife. He confessed that he struggled with this aspect of communication and felt unsure about how to approach it. When I inquired about his past attempts at criticism, he mentioned an incident from the previous week where his well-intentioned critique was met with resistance. As we delved deeper, I encouraged him to recall instances where he had critiqued his wife in a more successful manner.

He admitted that he hadn't quite mastered this skill, even though he understood the concept of beginning with a compliment. He knew that effective criticism involved initiating with a positive note before addressing the areas needing improvement. He cited his struggle to put this into practice, explaining that it felt foreign to him and not aligned with his true nature. Struggling to reconcile this, he expressed a sense of helplessness.

I drew from my memory a similar case I had encountered. Another person had shared a comparable concern about delivering criticism in a manner that felt incongruent with his identity. He had, however, excelled at this in a professional context. This individual, who worked in a messenger service, had to occasionally address concerns with his most important customer. Instead of coming across as critical, he approached it with appreciation.

When I asked this person how he managed to provide constructive feedback without causing offense, he revealed his approach. He would highlight the customer's significance, expressing gratitude for their loyalty and emphasizing his desire to maintain such a valuable partnership. He would then discuss the improvements he wished to see, framing it as a collaborative effort for better outcomes.

I relayed this anecdote to the person seeking advice, suggesting that the same approach could be applied within his marriage. I pointed out that this method of communication was not entirely foreign to him. After all, he interacted with clients regularly, using a similar technique to address concerns.

The concept of complimenting before criticizing wasn't alien; it was merely a different context. I emphasized that he possessed the ability to implement this strategy in his personal life as well. By recognizing his inherent capacity for such communication and acknowledging that he was not venturing into uncharted territory, he could overcome the discomfort he felt.

Drawing from his professional experience, I encouraged him to reflect on his role as a clothing store owner. Had he ever needed to address issues with his most significant customer? As expected, he had. In those instances, he had successfully employed the technique of praise followed by constructive feedback, all without causing offense. I highlighted that he was already adept at this skill, even if it had been compartmentalized to his business dealings.

Armed with this realization, the person began to see that the communication style he sought to adopt in his marriage wasn't a departure from his true self. Rather, it was a facet of his communication repertoire he had unconsciously segregated. Once he grasped that it was an extension of his established abilities, he started implementing it at home. The transformation was remarkable, leading to improved communication and a happier marriage.

In recounting this tale, I aimed to illustrate the power of recognizing our existing capabilities in different contexts. By bridging the gap between professional and personal spheres, he can more authentically and effectively enhance his relationships in both spheres.

Offer Encouragement Freed from Expectations

Another man I once met was also facing recurring conflict in his marriage. His wife doubted the genuineness of his compliments. His recounting of the conflict took me back to a moment when I was driving with a friend, and we were pulled over by a policeman for speeding. In our exchange with the officer, my friend sought to avoid a ticket, but his plea was met with a refusal. As the officer prepared the ticket, an idea struck me. I suggested that, instead of seeking leniency, my friend seize the opportunity to sincerely express his appreciation to the policeman. I advised him to convey his genuine admiration for the officer's selfless commitment to public safety and the risks he takes daily. By doing so, my friend's words would carry weight and authenticity, unmarred by an ulterior motive to evade the ticket.

My friend embraced the idea. When the officer returned with the ticket, my friend expressed his heartfelt gratitude for the officer's heroic dedication to ensuring public safety. The officer's response was deeply touching; he revealed the impact of my friend's genuine appreciation and decided to void the ticket.

Recalling this story, I shared it with the husband grappling with his wife's doubts about his sincerity. I explained that he could apply a similar principle to his situation. When his wife declined to do something for him and the request was no longer relevant, he could seize the moment to express his appreciation. By explaining that he wasn't upset about the unfulfilled request because he deeply valued all that she did for him, he would demonstrate the authenticity of his gratitude. This act of appreciation, divorced from immediate expectations, would resonate sincerely with his wife.

The husband put the advice into practice and later reported back with astonishment. His wife had finally recognized his genuine appreciation, allowing a breakthrough in their relationship. This instance underscored the potency of sincerity and the unexpected power of expressing gratitude at opportune moments. It taught both of them that authenticity transcends words, forging connections and understanding. The power of this technique lies in its ability to bridge the gap between intention and perception, infusing even the most ordinary interactions with genuine appreciation. It serves as a reminder that thoughtful gestures, unburdened by expectation, can build connections that words alone might struggle to achieve.

I once engaged in a thought-provoking conversation with an individual who habitually cast doubt upon my compliments, dismissing them as insincere gestures meant solely to boost their mood. In response, I offered a perspective that not only defended the authenticity of my words but also encouraged him to consider his reactions from a fresh angle.

I emphasized a fundamental truth: the intrinsic value of genuine compliments remains unaltered regardless of the speaker's underlying intentions. By focusing on the truthfulness of the compliment itself, I aimed to redirect his attention away from scrutinizing motivations and toward embracing the positive sentiments.

Moreover, I introduced an intriguing comparison that prompted him to reflect on his own behavior. I pointed out that his skepticism seemed to be reserved solely for compliments, whereas he rarely questioned the authenticity of criticism. This observation highlighted a potential double standard that might operate subconsciously. By underscoring this disparity, I intended to encourage a more equitable and balanced approach to evaluating feedback.

In essence, my response aimed not only to address his skepticism toward compliments but also to encourage introspection. By revealing the disparities in his reactions and biases, I hoped to empower him to cultivate a more open and receptive mindset—one that is equally discerning toward both praise and criticism. This process of self-awareness could pave the way for a healthier and more holistic perspective on the value of feedback.

The manner in which we articulate our encouragement, criticism, and concerns wields significant influence over the strength and vitality of our bonds. Genuine expressions of appreciation, when consistently embedded in our communication, contribute to the enrichment of our relationships. When we vocalize sincere praise, it becomes a source of affirmation, fostering an environment of mutual support and understanding.

Moreover, the reception of authentic encouragement is equally paramount. Being open to receiving genuine praise, acknowledging one another's accomplishments, and celebrating shared successes create a reciprocal cycle of positivity. It forms a foundation of trust and affirmation within relationships, nurturing an atmosphere where individuals feel valued and supported. In this dynamic exchange of encouragement, relationships flourish.

CHAPTER 16

FOSTER A HEALTHY ENVIRONMENT

See Challenges as Opportunities for Growth

Creating a healthy environment is the bedrock on which thriving relationships are built. Just as plants need fertile soil, relationships require a nourishing atmosphere to grow. This entails cultivating a space where open communication, trust, and mutual respect can take root. In a healthy environment, individuals feel safe expressing their thoughts and emotions, promoting a sense of security and understanding. By actively listening, validating each other's experiences, and offering support, we contribute to the emotional well-being of those around us. This positive environment becomes a sanctuary where relationships can weather challenges and celebrate successes.

Supporting the people we care about within this healthy environment is a testament to the strength of our connections. It involves not only being present during times of need but also actively contributing to each other's growth and happiness. Offering a listening ear, providing encouragement, and showing genuine interest in each other's aspirations nurtures a sense of companionship and shared goals. In this supportive environment, individuals are more likely to overcome obstacles, traverse uncertainties, and celebrate achievements together. Ultimately, fostering a healthy environment for our relationships is an investment in the well-being of both ourselves and those we care about, creating a foundation for lasting, meaningful connections.

Change the Environment to Increase Engagement

The principal of a prominent school contacted me with a pressing concern. He spoke of a particular student whose father held a strong philanthropic presence within the school community. This father's generosity was vast, with substantial donations enriching various school programs. However, the same couldn't be said for his son's academic performance. The student's grades were dishearteningly low, a stark contrast to the father's active involvement and financial support.

Troublingly, the father had begun placing blame on the school, asserting that the institution was not providing an adequate education for his child. This situation created a delicate balance between maintaining a supportive relationship with a major benefactor and addressing the educational needs of a struggling student.

As the principal and I discussed the case, it became evident that this particular student was not alone in facing concentration and academic challenges. The principal sought guidance not only in addressing this specific scenario but also in handling similar situations involving students with concentration difficulties.

Recognizing the complexity of the situation, I proposed a joint meeting with the teacher responsible for the struggling student. In the presence of the principal, we sat down with the teacher to gather insights that could shed light on the student's performance.

The teacher began by expressing his frustration, insisting that he shouldn't be blamed solely for the student's struggles. He even speculated that the student might be grappling with Attention Deficit Disorder (ADD).

Delving deeper, I probed the teacher to recall instances throughout the semester when he had successfully captured the student's attention. Surprisingly, he struggled to pinpoint any such moments. This predicament echoed a recurring theme that had emerged in previous chapters—the tendency for individuals to overlook their experiences, thus missing out on valuable insights.

Drawing parallels to other students in the classroom, I encouraged the teacher to explore whether there had been even a single occasion when the struggling student demonstrated focused attention. Despite initial reluctance and frustrated sighs, the teacher embarked on a journey of introspection. After several attempts, he managed to recollect an intriguing episode.

In this particular incident, the teacher had been resolute in motivating the student to excel in a subject. Determined to help the student achieve a good grade, the teacher had gone above and beyond to make the learning material captivating and engaging. The result was astounding—the student displayed a level of focus and concentration that was unprecedented. The outcome revealed that the student's capacity for concentration was not inherently impaired but rather influenced by external factors.

The discovery led to an intriguing insight: perhaps the student did not suffer from ADD but rather from what I termed "LED," or Lack Enjoyment Disorder. The notion resonated with the teacher, who had unknowingly stumbled upon the remedy for enhancing the student's concentration. This revelation emphasized that the key to nurturing concentration lay in establishing an environment of enjoyment and engagement.

The teacher's inquiry prompted further discussion about the concept of LED. I explained that just as an LED light source illuminates a room with vibrant energy, cultivating an environment where learning is enjoyable can illuminate a student's path to successful concentration. The teacher's expression transformed from skepticism to contemplation as he absorbed this fresh perspective on addressing concentration issues.

Amid our discussion, the principal interjected with curiosity, seeking more clarity on how the concept of LED could guide the school's approach. I emphasized that the heart of the matter was understanding that learning should not be a mere task but an experience that stimulates curiosity and nurtures genuine interest. The father's philanthropic intentions could be channeled into creating innovative and enjoyable learning opportunities for his son and other students.

In the end, what began as a dilemma rooted in accusations and frustration transformed into a collaborative journey toward understanding and solutions. The story of the struggling student illuminated a valuable lesson: the key to overcoming concentration challenges often lies in reimagining education as an engaging and joyful pursuit. As I left the school that day, I couldn't help but reflect on how a shift in perspective could benefit the lives of students and educators alike.

The environments in which we find ourselves have a great influence on our level of engagement and overall well-being. In the realm of relationships, the same principle holds true: fostering an environment that is both engaging and tailored to the individual contributes significantly to their success and happiness. Creating personalized spaces within relationships involves understanding the unique needs, aspirations, and challenges of each person involved. It entails a conscious effort to cultivate an atmosphere that encourages active participation, growth, and fulfillment. By prioritizing the creation of such environments, we lay the groundwork for flourishing connections, where individuals feel supported, motivated, and empowered to thrive.

Find Solutions to Make Healthy Choices Easier

In a charming suburban neighborhood, there lived a mother named Lisa, devoted to nurturing her two young children, Emma and Daniel. Amid the joys of parenting, Lisa often found herself faced with a common challenge: her children's unwavering preference for junk food over healthier choices.

Daniel, the older of the two, had developed a habit of gravitating toward sugary snacks and treats whenever mealtime came around. Lisa, like any concerned parent, worried about his nutrition and the effects of constant junk food consumption. She often found herself in a battle of wills, attempting to persuade Daniel to choose healthier alternatives.

One day, Lisa attended a local parenting workshop where she met a fellow mother who had once struggled with a similar dilemma. The woman shared her own experience of helping her child transition from a diet heavy in junk food to a more balanced one. Lisa was intrigued and eager to learn from the success story. As Lisa listened to the mother's journey, she recalled a similar situation with Emma. In the past, Emma had shown reluctance to eat vegetables, but Lisa had managed to turn the situation around by introducing creative ways to make healthy foods appealing. Drawing inspiration from her past experience, Lisa realized that she might be able to apply a similar approach with Daniel.

Determined to address the junk food challenge, Lisa reflected on her parenting journey and recognized that she had once found a way to make healthy choices exciting for her children. The memory of turning a potentially frustrating situation into a positive one filled her with renewed optimism.

The next afternoon, Lisa decided to embrace a new strategy. She invited Daniel to join her in the kitchen for a special "snack making adventure." As they assembled a colorful array of fruits, nuts, and whole-grain crackers, Lisa engaged Daniel in conversation about their favorite flavors and textures. With their homemade snack platter ready, Lisa and Daniel sat down to enjoy their creation. Daniel's eyes widened with curiosity as he sampled each item on the plate. Lisa's heart swelled with pride as she watched her son embrace the healthier options with genuine enthusiasm.

Over the following weeks, Lisa continued to introduce Daniel to a variety of tasty yet nutritious snack choices. They experimented with homemade versions of his favorite treats, replacing sugary ingredients with wholesome alternatives. With every small victory, Lisa's bond with Daniel grew stronger, and his attitude toward healthier foods began to shift.

One day at the park, Lisa shared her success story with a friend who was also grappling with a child's junk food preference. Encouraged by Lisa's experience, the friend decided to explore similar approaches at home. Lisa's realization that her past triumphs held the key to her current challenge became a guiding principle in her parenting journey. She learned that the answers she sought were often embedded in her own history as a parent, waiting to be unearthed and applied anew.

This story serves as a reminder that parenting is an ongoing process of learning and adaptation. By reflecting on our past successes, we can uncover solutions that resonate with our children's unique preferences and needs. Each accomplishment, no matter how small, contributes to a treasure trove of effective strategies that can be tailored to different parenting situations. By reflecting on past victories, we can discover innovative strategies to address present challenges. Through trial, error, and creative adaptation, we can cultivate an environment where everyday tasks are not just completed but transformed into opportunities for connection and growth.

Shifting perspectives toward healthier options and solutions often involves a strategic adjustment of both environments and language. The way we shape our surroundings and communicate directly influences people's responses and decisions. By making healthier choices more accessible and enjoyable, we can create an environment where well-being is not only prioritized but also celebrated. Language plays a crucial role in this transformation, as positive reinforcement and encouragement can significantly alter individuals' attitudes toward healthier alternatives. Through a combination of intentional environmental adjustments and empowering language, we can develop a culture where making health-conscious decisions becomes not just a choice but a natural and rewarding part of everyday life.

Build a Spirit of Cooperation

Once the parents of a family with ten children reached out to me with palpable distress, expressing their feelings of being overwhelmed and utterly lost in managing their children's behavior. The parents painted a vivid picture of daily struggles, citing disobedience, lack of cooperation, and the exhausting battle each night to put their kids to bed. Frustrated and disheartened, they felt that they were failing as parents and could not fathom a way out of their predicament.

As they poured out their feelings of helplessness, I could sense their desperation. They lamented the challenges they faced and recounted the times when their attempts at discipline and structure seemed to crumble. With a heavy heart, the mother admitted that she often found herself questioning her parenting abilities, wondering if she was failing her children.

In my effort to offer them guidance and a fresh perspective, I prompted them to consider something seemingly counterintuitive. I asked if they could recall a moment, even a singular one, where they had effectively managed their children's behavior or resolved a similar issue. Their reaction was a mix of skepticism and doubt. They were convinced that their struggles had been consistent and that they had never truly succeeded in overcoming such challenges.

Undeterred, I encouraged them to take a moment to reflect, to search their memories for any glimmer of success. I assured them that often our recollections can surprise us, revealing instances we had momentarily forgotten or underestimated. The parents hesitated, racking their brains, and as they dug deeper, a glimmer of realization began to surface.

Eventually, the mother spoke up. She recounted a specific episode when she was on the phone with a friend while her child's disruptive behavior became evident. Her friend, attuned to the situation, offered a piece of advice from an expert: "Remind your child of their goodness and your love for them, and let them know that going to bed would make you happy." This strategy aimed to appeal to the child's self-concept as a "good kid" and tap into their desire to bring joy to their mother.

With a renewed sense of hope, the mother decided to give this approach a shot. She conveyed her love and confidence in her child's goodness and gently suggested that going to bed at the right time would be a wonderful way to make her happy. The result was astonishing: a marked shift in behavior. The bedtime battles diminished, and a spirit of cooperation emerged.

As I listened to her share this experience, I couldn't help but emphasize the significance of what had just unfolded. It was a tangible demonstration of a pattern that had repeatedly emerged in my interactions with individuals facing challenges. Despite initial skepticism, most people had, indeed, encountered and successfully mediated similar situations in the past.

I guided her to recognize the potency of her own experiences and insights. I pointed out that, quite often, the solutions we need are hidden within our own memories and past triumphs. Just as the mother had instinctively tapped into a forgotten strategy, she too possessed a wellspring of knowledge and creativity within herself.

With a newfound sense of empowerment, the parents listened attentively. The same couple who had entered the conversation in despair was now visibly lighter, as if a weight had been lifted. I reminded them that our own experiences are not just anecdotes; they are valuable tools in navigating life's challenges. Armed with this understanding, they were equipped to address their children's behavior with renewed confidence.

As we concluded our conversation, the parents expressed a blend of gratitude and amazement. They marveled at the idea that they held within them the potential to resolve their struggles all along. What had seemed like an insurmountable problem was now reframed as an opportunity for growth and transformation. This encounter left a lasting impression on them, serving as a testament to the power of tapping into our own history and experiences to find solutions to the challenges we face.

Fostering a spirit of cooperation in relationships involves cultivating a language of understanding, empathy, and encouragement. By communicating expectations with empathy, we create an environment where individuals feel acknowledged and supported. When language is framed positively, with a focus on encouragement rather than criticism, it builds a sense of collective growth. This approach encourages everyone involved to thrive, promoting a cooperative spirit where challenges are faced together, and successes are celebrated collaboratively. Through mindful and supportive communication, relationships can evolve into spaces where individuals not only meet expectations but surpass them, driven by a shared sense of encouragement and a genuine desire to see one another succeed.

In both professional and personal spheres, we wield a considerable influence in shaping the environments around us. While it may seem daunting to change external factors, the power lies in how we approach, communicate, and interact with others. In professional settings, the language we use, the support we provide, and the collaborative spirit contributes significantly to the work atmosphere. A positive and encouraging approach can transform a workplace into an environment where creativity flourishes, ideas are freely shared, and individuals feel empowered to contribute their best.

Similarly, in personal relationships, the way we communicate, show empathy, and express encouragement plays a pivotal role in shaping the emotional environment.

A few years ago, I faced a challenging case where I believed the person needed medication alongside therapy. Seeking insight, I reached out to the esteemed psychiatrist, Dr. Alan Manevitz. Beyond his renowned expertise, he proved to be one of the kindest and most humble individuals I've ever known. During our discussion, after offering his brilliant assessment, he asked, "Rabbi Stein, what's your opinion?" Hearing those words from a legendary doctor who has saved thousands of lives throughout the years and developed extraordinary techniques to help people had a profound impact on me, providing a momentum I find hard to put into words.

By establishing a climate of trust, understanding, and support, we create spaces where individuals can grow, express themselves authentically, and feel secure. Acknowledging the influence we possess allows us to be intentional about creating environments that uplift and inspire, ultimately contributing to positive transformations in both our professional and personal spheres.

SIMPLE SOLUTIONS TO COMPLEX PROBLEMS

As we face each unique problem in our daily lives, it might feel as though, because of the distinct context, we've never faced similar challenges before. We might even feel lost and stuck with no idea for how to move forward. But as you've seen throughout the course of these chapters, there are common threads in all the problems we've faced, especially within the realms of identity, emotions, and interpersonal conflict. Through mindfully looking to our past, we can uncover blueprints for how to navigate our present and future challenges.

I once encountered an individual who confessed to having a persistent tendency to give up on challenges, driven by the belief that solutions, even if they existed, were bound to be overly complex. Initially, I found myself grappling with how to alter this mindset. Then, a memory surfaced—recollections of a speech I once delivered on a similar subject.

In that speech, I shared a story of a magician renowned for his skill in escaping from cages. Regardless of the complexity, he could extricate himself within moments. However, there was one instance that posed a formidable challenge. Placed within a seemingly inescapable cage, he had a mere minute to decipher his way out. As time dwindled, he struggled, fifty seconds passing in vain. With only ten seconds remaining, a realization struck: he discovered that the door was unlocked. Swiftly, he turned the knob and calmly walked out.

The essence of my speech was to encourage the audience to adopt a different perspective. Instead of surrendering due to an assumed complexity, explore simpler alternatives first. In the magician's case, the obvious solution was the open door—a solution overlooked due to the assumption that the situation must be intricate.

Drawing from this narrative, I imparted a similar message to the individual struggling with his inclination to give up prematurely. I highlighted the importance of considering straightforward solutions before labeling challenges as insurmountable. The metaphor of the open door resonated with him, prompting a change in his perspective. He later shared that he had undergone a complete transformation in how he approached challenges, emphasizing a newfound willingness to explore simpler solutions before conceding defeat.

This experience illustrated the power of relatable anecdotes in reshaping perspectives. The magician's story not only captivated my audience during the speech but also served as a practical tool for instigating positive change in the individual I encountered. It underscored the significance of questioning assumptions and considering alternatives before surrendering to the perceived complexity of a situation.

In moments of distress, our focus often narrows to the immediate problem at hand. However, when we widen our perspective and draw from our own history, we unlock a wealth of solutions. It was a reminder that resilience, creativity, and growth were all innately human qualities, waiting to be rediscovered.

A relative once called me seeking advice on finding the right person for an important task. Initially stumped, I struggled to figure out a solution. However, a past experience resurfaced in which someone had asked me a similar question. I had advised her to treat her phone's contact list like a comprehensive directory of connections. By scrolling through her contacts, one name would spark memories of others, ultimately leading to the right person or someone who could point her in the right direction.

Recalling this advice, I shared it with my relative. The results were even more impressive than I had anticipated. This situation serves as a reminder that our own forgotten insights can be surprisingly effective when applied in different contexts. The simple approach of leveraging our own experiences can lead to remarkable solutions, as demonstrated by the positive outcome my relative experienced.

Every experience, triumph, and setback we encounter contributes to a store of wisdom that can guide us through the challenges of today. As we navigate the complexities of personal identity, emotional landscapes, and relationships, our past experiences become invaluable compasses, offering insights into effective strategies and cautionary tales of what may not work.

Introspection, the art of delving into the recesses of our own minds, becomes a crucial tool in this journey. By reflecting on our past, we unearth the lessons buried within the folds of time. In the realm of personal identity, our journey unfolds as a narrative shaped by numerous decisions, encounters, and self-discoveries. Through introspection, we can trace the roots of our beliefs, understand the evolution of our values, and discern the driving forces that have propelled us forward. Armed with this self-awareness, we gain clarity on our authentic selves and the principles that form the bedrock of our identities.

Emotional landscapes, often intricate and challenging, also benefit from the light of introspection. By revisiting past emotional upheavals and triumphs, we gain a nuanced understanding of our responses, coping mechanisms, and triggers. This self-awareness equips us to navigate the labyrinth of emotions with greater resilience and efficacy. We learn to decipher the subtle cues our emotions provide, enabling us to respond thoughtfully to the challenges presented by today's intricate emotional terrain.

Moreover, the realm of relationships, with its intricate dance of connections and communications, is enriched through introspection. Examining past relationships, both successful and challenging, allows us to discern patterns, understand our contributions to dynamics, and identify areas for growth. The mistakes of yesterday become guideposts for today, steering us away from pitfalls and toward healthier connections. Introspection enables us to approach relationships with a deeper understanding of ourselves and others, promoting empathy, effective communication, and the ability to forge meaningful connections.

Our experiences offer knowledge that extends beyond the confines of specific situations. The strategies we employed to overcome obstacles, the resilience we exhibited in times of adversity, and the insights gained from our triumphs collectively serve as a toolkit for addressing the challenges of today. Whether facing uncertainties, professional dilemmas, or personal tribulations, the lessons learned from our unique life journeys provide a robust foundation for devising effective strategies.

As we confront the problems of the present, the wisdom garnered from introspection becomes a source of empowerment. It reminds us that we are not navigating uncharted territories but drawing from a well of experiences that have shaped us. This recognition fosters confidence and resilience, allowing us to face today's challenges with a seasoned perspective. By embracing the lessons of our past, we embark on a continuous journey of growth and adaptation, harnessing the richness of our experiences to navigate the complexities of the present and shape a more enlightened future.

As you journeyed through the pages of this book, I hope you felt the stirrings of insight and the gentle nudges of inspiration. Books are more than a collection of words; they are vessels carrying the potential for transformation, a journey into the landscapes of one's own mind and heart. Now, as you stand at the intersection of these thoughts and your own lived experiences, I encourage you to carry the wisdom you've gathered into your life.

Each chapter of your story is an opportunity for growth, and within the folds of your own narrative lies the power to face uncertainties that lie ahead. Just as the characters in a book face their trials and emerge stronger, you too have everything you need within the chapters of your own existence.

Apply the lessons you've gleaned from these pages with intentionality. Life's challenges are not roadblocks but steps, guiding you toward a deeper understanding of yourself and the world around you. Reflect on the narratives of your past, the victories, the defeats, and the quiet moments of resilience. It is within these very experiences that you'll find the tools, insights, and strength to face whatever challenges may come your way.

Remember, life's most profound lessons often unfold in the quiet spaces of introspection and self-discovery. As you continue your journey, let the echoes of the stories you've encountered here serve as companions, offering guidance and encouragement. Trust in your own narrative, for within it lies the extraordinary capacity to shape a story of resilience, growth, and authenticity.

May you find the courage to embrace the unwritten chapters with curiosity and the conviction to craft a narrative that reflects the beauty and strength inherent in your unique story.

ABOUT
THE AUTHOR

Rabbi Joel Stein, a prominent figure and bestselling author in the Orthodox Jewish community, demonstrated remarkable achievements early in life. By the age of twenty-two, he delivered profound lectures on halachic rulings, reaching tens of thousands of listeners. At twenty-six, he authored insightful commentary on the entire Talmud. Throughout his years as a rabbi, people sought his guidance for a range of struggles, including complex mental challenges. Rabbi Stein surpassed expectations, offering assistance where even the most seasoned experts had faltered. Pioneering revolutionary techniques for resolving psychological issues, he successfully mediated numerous multimillion-dollar disputes that had been deadlocked for decades. His innovative ideas also paved the way for legendary success in the world of business.

ENDNOTES

1 | "Sobibor Extermination Camp." Wikipedia, January 1, 2024. https:// en.wikipedia.org/wiki/Sobibor_extermination_camp.

2 | Borowski, Susan. "The Brilliant and Tortured World of Nikola Tesla." American Association for the Advancement of Science (AAAS), 2012. https://www.aaas.org/brilliant-and-tortured-world-nikola-tesla.

3 | James, Brian. "Nikola Tesla Patents: The Patents of the Godfather of Electricity." Electrical Apparatus, November 9, 2018. https://www.electricalapparatus.net/ nikola-tesla-patents-amazing-patents-godfather-electricity/.

4 | "Nikola Tesla." OCDUK. Accessed January 10, 2024. https://www. ocduk.org/ocd/history-of-ocd/nikola-tesla/#:~:text=He%20also%20 became%20obsessed%20with,every%20meal%20using%2018%20 napkins.